Gon

Wild in th
Fells of the Lake District

Also by Steven Freeman

Black Sail
The Purple House
Down West

Gone Feral

Wild in the Woods and Fells of the Lake District

Steven Freeman

Published by Outgate Press, 2019
outgatepress@outlook.com

ISBN 978-1-5272-4441-2

To be most alive is to be most free
is to be most wild.
Jay Griffiths
Wild: An Elemental Journey

Enveloped by Nature

Rain patters on the tarpaulin above my head as I sit in the camping chair, listening to the peaceful coo-cooing of a wood pigeon, the twitter of songbirds and the constant gentle sound of running stream water. It's a cool damp morning and I'm sitting in the middle of a wood run wild, surrounded by beech, birch, sycamore, oak, hazel and holly. This is an *ancient* woodland, a bit of wildwood, a fragment of the original temperate rainforest that once covered the entire Lake District. At one time it must have been managed, and you can see where the hazels and beeches were coppiced, their clusters of pale poles sprouting from near the bases of the trunks. Also, in places there's an occasional old stake in the ground, surrounded by black plastic mesh to protect a planted sapling that never came to anything. Man's efforts to manage and control Nature here have been abandoned and the wood has been allowed to revert to its wild state. Derelict, ungoverned, it's a little patch of anarchy, freedom and vitality in a landscape that is otherwise farmed, pruned, castrated and tamed. Here there is a healthy wild matrix of life, a host of different species co-operatively cohabiting a vibrant ecosystem. I stare into the trees, at the upright trunks and the limbs branching off at all angles, intertwining with each other and forming a dense web higher up in the leafy green canopy, but with gaps – windows to the grey sky above, and to the grey world outside my green sylvan idyll. Tangles of ivy and honeysuckle tendrils dangle from the criss-cross jumble of branches, the honeysuckle giving off a delicious sickly-sweet sexual fragrance like ylang ylang or vanilla ice cream. Fallen dead boughs have lodged amongst live branches, stopped in their fall to the ground by outstretched limbs and soldered to them with lush green moss. And on the ground there's a rich mix of grasses, ferns, bluebells, ramsons, dog mercury, and many other species I don't know. It's a jungle of abundant green life here, a far cry from the man-made, straight-lined, built-on, paved and tarmacked-over grey environment of the town. It's a habitat I share with birds, squirrels, roe deer, beetles, caterpillars and countless other creatures. Enveloped by Nature, it's a good place to contemplate – if I can engage my mind with my woodland environment and not be too distracted by worldly cares of jobs and money or the practical difficulties of living like this.

Why *am* I living like this? Basically because I needed somewhere to live in this area but I couldn't afford a room. I didn't have much choice. I've got a job in town, working in one of the outdoor shops. I don't like the job, but again, I didn't have much choice. I needed some sort of job to survive, and it was all I could get. I quite like living in the wood though. I like living close to Nature, away from the crowds, the busyness and the noise of town. Here there is stillness, quietness, save for the gentle raindrop pattering, the stream and the birdsong. Also the flutter of wings of a little wren that nests nearby in the root base of a fallen beech tree. She flits about the low branches and skips across the ground, looking for morsels perhaps, or maybe just exercising, playing. But then the quietness is shattered by the roar of two low-flying jets, invisible through the green canopy and thick grey cloud, but very much up there on an exercise, preparing for war, whilst we creatures of the wood want only peace. Silence returns, and the wren re-appears out of her nest, just a few feet away – my next door neighbour. She looks at me and I look at her and talk to her – 'Hello mate, good morning to you. What's that in your beak?' She jumps around a bit, weighing up the situation, but she's getting used to my presence here now and carries on doing her thing regardless.

I am looking for a room, but I don't think I want to live in town, which is where the rented rooms mostly are. Also I can't really afford to pay the going rate in rent round here. I used to have a room in the house down the track, the house to which this wood belongs, but that's not possible anymore. I used to lodge there with Dorothy, who's old and disabled and needs some help with fetching and carrying, wood-cutting, fire laying, gardening and cooking. I worked for about ten hours a week for her in lieu of rent, whilst also working at the forest shop in Grizedale. That was a couple of years ago and I had the attic room above the kitchen, 'the den', with its separate entrance up the stone steps. But the room is now occupied by her long-term helper Harry, and the other attic room in the house is used by short-term helpers who usually come to stay for just a few weeks. Anyway, Dorothy said I could camp in the wood until such time as I can find a room elsewhere. I can also use the house for showers, the washing machine and drinking water, but for this she expects me to do a few odd jobs by way of exchange. It's an arrangement that suits me for the time being.

And so I set up camp here in the wood a few weeks ago. I spent a little time looking round for a good spot and had originally intended to pitch up on the other side of the track, where a faint path leads to a flat area near the field boundary, but it didn't feel private enough and it didn't feel right somehow. So I explored some more and found this place, which is pretty much in the middle of the wood. There was no path going this way through the trees, just leaf litter and twigs and the odd fallen branch. The ground dropped down to the stream and then rose on the other side to a small flattish clearing carpeted in bluebells. I knew immediately this was the place to set up camp. And so I pitched my Vaude backpacking tent on the highest flattest patch, below a couple of small beech trees. First I put down a tarpaulin and lay on this to make sure it was level and to check for lumps of roots or twigs or stones. It took me a little while to get the best position, with the door of the tent opening onto the clearing. This is my sleeping tent or 'bedroom'. Inside I've got an old woollen blanket spread out over the floor for a bit of insulation, and then my inflatable mat. At first I slept in my sleeping bag, but I've started using a duvet, which is much more comfortable. Next to it I pitched my old ridge tent, which I use for storage of food and other stuff, and to the side of that I strung up a tarpaulin from low beech branches at an angle so that the rain can run off. Below the tarp I've got a large camping table, the folding armchair, and also a small wooden table with my large one-ring gas stove sitting on it. This is my kitchen, dining and living 'room', and in front of this I've constructed a ring-of-stones fireplace. I'm quite pleased with the set-up, which looks and feels like a longish-term living arrangement, rather than a fleeting recreational camp. I've been here for something like three weeks now and so I'm feeling quite settled in. When I first moved here the weather was dry and sunny. That was mid-May, and there was a thick carpet of bluebells in this little clearing. But since then there's been quite a bit of wet weather, the bluebell flowers have gone and the grass has been trampled by my comings and goings, so that the ground is getting rather bare and muddy in places. I've been putting down pieces of cardboard here and there but could do with something more substantial as the cardboard soon starts to disintegrate after it's rained and I've walked over it a few times. Anyway, overall I'm quite pleased with my campsite, and I reckon I'd rather live like this than rent a room in a shared house in town.

It's not perfect though, and as I sit in my chair, staring into the trees, the peace and quiet is again violated, this time by the sound of banging car doors and coarse loud human voices just a few hundred yards up the lane. And then the sound of a chainsaw buzzing and droning as it cuts through some timber – perhaps the limb of a living tree being severed. And, although I can't see the world outside the wood, I can certainly hear it and it isn't far away. My little patch of wildness and my peace and quiet are fragile, vulnerable, and I wish I were further away from human society. Anyway, the noise has galvanised me into action, and reminded me that I could do with cutting some firewood before I set off to work in the shop.

The rain has stopped now, the sun is shining tentatively through the trees, and the forecast is for a dry, warm and sunny day. I put the kettle on for another coffee and get the bow saw from inside the flysheet of the storage tent, where it rests on a small pile of sawn logs. In so doing I disturb a small rodent – a vole I think. I say 'hello', as I do to most animals, but he scampers away through the tent door and into the trees. There wasn't time to for me to explain that I didn't mind him being there, but that I'd be in and out every day, re-arranging the logs where he'd found shelter. Anyway, I take the saw and set to work on the fallen beech tree at the edge of the clearing.

Sawing through some of the smaller branches first, I don't know when the tree fell or how long it's been 'dead' – if indeed it is entirely dead. Trees may topple over, but still have plenty of life in them, as evidenced by new shoots that spring forth from apparently dead limbs. I think sometimes it can be difficult to kill a mature tree, as it has such a strong core life-force that it keeps regenerating. This old beech is more dead than alive though. The branches that I saw through are not exactly 'seasoned', but they're not green either, and they'll make half-decent firewood. I push and pull the sharp-toothed steel blade back and forth through the soft wood in a simple and satisfying motion that's a good bit of physical exercise with a practical purpose. Pale sawdust collects around the cut and falls to the wet grass. As I get close to the bottom of the branch I feel the tension as it bends, and I work the blade with extra vigour until I'm all the way through and the limb thuds softly to the ground. And then I saw through another, and another.

The kettle whistles on the hob and so I break off to make another instant coffee in my green plastic mug. I love the taste of coffee in the morning. I suppose it's just what I've become used to. I take a couple of sips and then return to my log-sawing. I've warmed up with quite a few smallish ones, so now I'm going to work on some bigger stuff. There's the stump-end of a bough I was working on the other day, and I'll carry on from where I left off. There's maybe three more chunky logs to be had from that limb. And so I saw away, working hard but steadily for a few minutes, until I'm all the way through and the first log drops. I pick it up and there's quite a bit of weight to it − still quite a bit of water content, although I know it'll burn okay once the fire is hot. I'm sweating a bit now and I take off my fleece, drape it over the chair and gulp down some more coffee. And then I work on sawing the other two logs. Manual work like this makes me feel good. It's good to exercise the muscles and get the blood pumping round the body. A combination of this sawing and the coffee-drinking has also had the effect of making me want to empty my bowel, and so I break off to fetch the toilet paper and shovel from the storage tent and set off into the wood towards the big holly tree.

This is the way I usually go – towards a boggy area well away from camp, through a jungle of tendrils and low hazel branches. The way is marked first by an old flat label-less glass bottle, half sunk into the ground, then by an old crushed and rusty Carling Black Label lager can. Evidence of previous campers perhaps – from decades ago. I could pick up these old pieces of rubbish and bin them, but I like them being there as markers on my way through the 'jungle'. Beyond the old lager can the ground gets softer and is boggy in places – a good area for digging holes to bury my faeces. I get to a suitable spot and see a deer not far away, a bit further towards the fence. It turns and sees me, then bounds off, its high-viz white rump bouncing up and down as it runs through the trees. I take the shovel, which is actually a collapsible snow shovel but ideal for this task and start to dig a hole in the ground. The shovel edge is pointed and quite sharp, so it's good for digging small holes. The earth is damp and soft and gives way easily. And as I excavate the hole I get the rich earthy smell of the soil. A little deeper and some murky water oozes through the humus, pooling at the bottom. I drop my trousers and underpants, squat down and extrude a long healthy turd that falls neatly into the hole, coiling like a Cumberland sausage. My bladder then relaxes and I urinate, still squatting, over the gently steaming stool. Then I take some tissue, wipe myself and throw the dirty tissue into the hole. And there's something very satisfying about going for a shit in a hole in the woods, rather than on a ceramic 'throne' flush toilet in a house. I stand up and pull up my pants and trousers, then I use the shovel to replace the earth and bury the turd in its six-inch deep grave. Finally I mark the spot with a cross of twigs lying flat on the ground − so that I know not to dig in that spot again. And then I walk back to camp, snapping off some dead hazel poles for kindling on the way. I rinse the shovel in the beck and wipe it clean and dry on a mossy tree trunk. It's now 9.40am and time I headed into Ambleside to work at the shop.

Objectives of the Day

The traffic on the road isn't too bad, it being still a bit early for most of the tourists, although when I get to Ambleside it does get busier. I need to start cycling to work more, but that wouldn't combine well with my after work runs and swims from Rydal. And today I'm definitely planning on a run, then a swim in Rydal Water. I drive up Compston Road and get into the right-hand lane to turn up to Market Cross, the hub of this honeypot town – or 'village', if you prefer. Opposite the old stone war memorial is a courtyard area surrounded by shops, and I work at one of the shops in there. There are a couple of staff parking spaces just a bit further on, and that's where I park this morning, opposite the back entrance to the Queens Hotel.

The shop is like so many other outdoor shops in the Lakes – selling outdoor clothing and equipment to walkers and to moochers who like to look the part. It's at the lower end, the 'budget' end of the market, and so attracts customers who are not serious outdoor types, but who might go for low level walks, or maybe just bimble about town. It's a big corporate company, so it treats its staff poorly and is constantly running ever-changing promotions to attract customers through the doors and get them to buy the 'cheap' product, which is mostly of poor quality and isn't even worth the promotional half price, never mind the 'top ticket' price, which is the price it was theoretically sold at for a couple of weeks online, or in some of their stores.

As I enter the shop, manager Sharon and assistant Paul – who will have both started at 9am – are stood side by side behind the counter, but they don't even see me as they're engrossed with their smartphones, giggling at something on a screen. I walk quickly up the stairs, drop off my rucksack in the stock room and go back down to clock on at the till. It's 10am precisely. Today I will work 'til 4pm, so not exactly a full day. My shifts and hours are variable, depending on 'the needs of the business', and some weeks I may work about thirty hours, and other weeks it may only be about twenty. I'm only contracted to four hours a week, and it may drop to this in the winter, if I'm still here – which I almost certainly won't be. I'm only paid the so-called 'National Living Wage', which of course is hardly a real living wage, even if I were to be working full-time hours. But with camping in the wood I have no rent to pay, so it should be survivable, once the money actually comes through at the end of the month.

Sharon goes through the shop targets and objectives for the day. We have shop targets to strive for every day – key performance indicators or 'KPIs', which relate to total sales, average customer spend, items per basket and the number of transactions per number of people who pass over the threshold (where they are counted by an electronic sensor). The KPI scores have to be emailed to head office at the end of each day, and if we are not hitting our targets the Area Manager will want to know why and will pressure Sharon to come up with strategies to achieve the targets. There's a daily sales target for the whole store, and each individual team member has their own target, based on the number of hours they are working that day. Sharon shows me a sheet of paper with my target for the day (£350), and I have to sign this to show that I understand what is expected of me. Also on this sheet are the objectives of the day, which read: 'Thorough tidy of stock on the shop floor', 'Complete delivery', 'Engage with customers', 'Strive for add-on sales' and 'Have fun!'. I'll do the best I can, but it's unlikely that I'm going to have much fun.

She switches on the music system, and the awful *muzak* starts. It's compulsory that we play this – a compilation of unsigned artists singing formulaic crap. And as the day goes on, wave after wave of customers, mostly just mooching about aimlessly, or maybe hunting for a bargain, will come in – the happy shoppers visiting the familiar high street chain stores, the churches of materialistic acquisitive consumer culture, reassured by the smile of the sales assistant and the awful clichéd songs that constantly play from the speakers – songs about 'love' sung by warbling auto-tuned singers saying how they 'feel so high I could touch the sky', how they will never leave their partner, or how 'everything's going to be all right'.

Anyway, Sharon says she wants to go up to the office with me to 'have a little chat'. And so we go upstairs and sit in the tiny office area, which is also a footwear stock room and very untidy. She's quite a sexy girl with lots of blonde hair, curvy, buxom, though pasty and not the slightest bit outdoorsy. She's got a nice big smile, which won me over when I applied for the job, but she's not smiling this morning. After the initial 'How's it going?' she gets to the point and tells me she's not happy with my performance so far and may have to 'let me go' if I don't improve over the next week or so. It seems the issue that's got her back up is that I didn't stay behind later than my scheduled hours the other delivery day, to finish tagging and hanging a big box of stock. I was due to finish at 4pm, and at five minutes to the hour she sent Paul up to tell me that I wasn't allowed to go until I'd completed the box, which would've taken at least an hour. I wasn't happy about that, so I left at 4pm on the dot, saying I was sorry but I couldn't stay as I had things to do. Sharon says that she needs staff who are prepared to 'flex up' hours 'to meet the needs of the business' etc. This is so often how it works in these part-time shop jobs. They expect you to 'flex up' at a moment's notice but may also flex your hours *down* with little notice to give more hours to their favoured members of staff, or because of some instruction from head office about the need to reduce staff hours. I explain to Sharon that her demand that I stay later at a moment's notice, via messenger Paul, was unfair and unprofessional, but I can tell that she's already made up her mind that she doesn't like me – basically because I won't always jump when she tells me to. She's the manager, she likes to control people and her ego can't take it if anyone questions the way she does things. She's little more than a kid, with no people management skills and few shop management skills either. She's only been in the role for a few weeks, and she's struggling to cope with it. I could complain to the Area Manager, but he'd probably side with her, or at least give her the benefit of the doubt. I'd be better just looking for another job.

After our meeting she instructs me to sweep the floor, tidy up the stock on display and serve customers until the delivery arrives around early lunchtime. It's 10.30am now, there are some customers browsing in the shop, and I'm wondering why she or Paul didn't sweep the floor first thing, but I don't mind doing it – a basic housekeeping task that is meaningful in its simplicity. There's some job satisfaction to be had from sweeping up the dust and polyester fluff on the wooden floor into a neat pile, then brushing it into a dustpan and emptying it in a bin. But as for tidying the stock – I find this a soul-destroying task because it's never-ending, and also because the standards of presentation are disproportionate to the quality of the product. An instruction has come through from head office, detailing exactly how clothing should be displayed on the shop floor, and of course they want it to be immaculate. But it only takes one customer to rummage through the jackets and destroy the display effect, so that you have to do it all over again.

When the delivery arrives around early lunchtime I make a start on checking this off in a back room but have to keep breaking off to serve customers. Sharon goes on her lunch, Paul goes upstairs to serve a customer with boots and I need to stay on the shop floor rather than being tucked away with the delivery.

Finally, at 2pm I'm permitted to take my half-hour lunch break. First I go to The Picnic Box for my cheese ploughman's roll, then I walk up North Road and Peggy Hill to a wooden bench near the old St. Anne's Church, where I sit in the sun to eat. But I have to keep an eye on my watch – it's all a bit rushed, and before long I have to get up and go back down the hill to clock in at the shop for the afternoon shift.

Back in the retail courtyard tourists wander round with a cardboard cup of Costa coffee in one hand and a smartphone in the other, wondering what to spend their money on next. There are a dozen or so other coffee shops in town but most people seem to flock to Costa because it's familiar, nay ubiquitous, on every high street in every town. People know what they are going to get – something standardised, mass-produced and *branded*, which is reassuring to them. They walk through town with their Costa cup – which will end up with all the hundreds of others in the public litter bins or on the pavements. They love these familiar corporate businesses which have taken over our town centres. Shopping is Britain's favourite pastime, and perhaps this is what taking part in society largely consists of these days: shopping at familiar high street stores. This town of Ambleside used to be more of a characterful place, a community of locals with useful independent shops, as well as being a tourist destination and base for fell-walking adventures. Nowadays it's just for the tourists and, as *The Rough Guide to The Lake District* put it: 'More a retail experience than a Lakeland town.' Mind you, these days most towns and cities are pretty much just 'retail experiences'.

Released from Captivity

Running now along a stony bridleway from Rydal, I descend through some trees to a gate in the wall, and then beyond the gate I'm in the bright late-afternoon sunshine, looking down at the inviting sparkling water of the lake. There are a couple of swimmers, their clothes left on the big log on the beach by the wall. I'll go for a swim from there myself later, but first I'll run for a few miles, or do as much as I can. After a day in the shop my body and spirit feel drained. My legs are leaden, but I can force them to run to some extent. I am a runner, after all – a *fell*-runner, no less, although sometimes I don't feel like one. I'm planning to run a fifty mile round of the fells in just about a week's time, so I need to at least keep my legs turning over. I've done a lot of training for it over the spring, so I am basically fit for it, but I need to maintain that fitness by getting out for a decent fell run every few days, or else I'll lose it.

This bright sunny weather is inspiring and I make an effort, trotting along the stony track, breaking into a walk up the difficult stony section up towards the caves, then trotting again along the narrow winding path and progressing upwards to Loughrigg Terrace.

This is a very popular route with walkers, but at this time of day (5pm) there aren't too many people about. It's a beautiful area, with views northwards to Grasmere, and eastwards to the wooded slopes leading up to Fairfield, and it's just a five-minute drive from Ambleside to where I parked my car on the lane that leads from Pelter Bridge. Being able to get out into this, 'the great outdoors', after a day in the shop makes life worth living. This *is* living, whereas working in the shop is a living death. I'd like to go up onto Loughrigg this evening, but my legs have been leadened and my spirit deadened by a day of corporate retail wage slavery. I'm about to turn back at the top of the terrace but then decide to force myself up the rock staircase to Loughrigg. Sometimes it's possible to break through the tiredness and get into a run.

My body doesn't want to be doing this, but my mind overrides it and commands it to do what I know will be good for it. The change of gear as I stride up this steep path helps the process. It's too steep for running but I can power-walk up here, my head bent to the task, hands on knees, my heart and lungs working as hard as if I was running, the red oxygenated blood pumping round the system, charging my internal battery, my bodily electricity, building up a charge, transforming and increasing my internal voltage to the point where the indicator on the meter moves into a positive, a high position, a place where I've got the bit between my teeth and I've got the daemon back inside of me. And as I feel myself bite I am back to my true nature, which is red in tooth and Mudclaw.

Sweating, I pause to take off my tee-shirt and stow it in the bum-bag. It's good to feel the afternoon sun on my bare back, and I feel more the feral animal, released from captivity, at home and at one with the fell. Onwards I push upwards. Push, push, hard, strong, fluid, rhythmic, present, one-pointed. Lifting the legs, feet onto boulders, now using the hands and feeling the warm dry rock, then the gradient eases off and I break into a jog and keep it going up the final grassy slope to the top of the fell, where a cluster of walkers are admiring the view westwards. And without a pause I round the trig point and drop down a steep grassy slope in a different direction to the one I came up. I'm heading for High Close and Red Bank, this bit being on the route of my round. I find the narrow path and drop steeply through the bracken, keeping the rhythm going as I dance downwards through the greenery, keeping my balance and keeping the forward momentum going as I finally drop down to the road, where I turn right and jog along the tarmac for a bit before going through a gate on my right and following a track that brings me back to the top of the Loughrigg Terrace. And from here I run back down the way I came up, letting gravity pull me down, and pushing a bit as well – to pick up speed and enjoy the play of running downhill, watching my feet and negotiating the rocks by adjusting my stride, jumping here and there and dancing my way down to the lake shore by a different path, so that I run along the pebbly beach by the water's edge – and I'm ready for a swim.

At the beach with the big log the other swimmers have just got dressed and gone, so I have the place to myself. I simply take off my bum bag and walk straight into the cold water in my running shoes. The water is cold, and when it reaches genital level I stop to adjust to the temperature, splashing the water over my chest and face. And then I take a few more steps on the rocky lake bed, a little deeper into the water, finally taking the plunge, submerging myself up to my neck. There's a momentary shock, but it doesn't last long, and now it feels good to be in the water. I start to swim breast stroke, westwards towards the still-bright, though fairly low sun. And I needed this perhaps as much as the run. The cold water is invigorating, and the cares of the day are washed away. I'm baptising myself, making myself anew in Nature's own swimming pool. A couple of dog walkers walk along the shore, and on the other side, in the distance, the motor traffic on the A591 goes past but doesn't bother me. One evening I'd like to swim to the island in the middle of the lake, but today, as usual, I'm just going to swim parallel to the shore, towards the sun for a few hundred yards, then swim back the same way.

Out of the water, I jog back along the track to the car, where I dry myself, get changed and then drive the short distance to The Badger Bar, where I order a pint of Badger Pale Ale. After the day in the shop, the run and the swim, I'm more than ready for this. I take it outside to the picnic tables by the roadside and watch the traffic go by as I gulp the beer down quickly. It's refreshing and relaxing, and I need another one already, so I go back to the bar, which is an old-fashioned wooden-floored pub attached to the Glen Rothay Hotel. 'Another pint of Badger and a packet of salted nuts, please,' I say to Andy, the barman, as I hand him the empty glass. 'By golly, that can't have touched the sides,' he says, and as he pulls me another one I look at the little sign hanging behind the bar which says 'Today's soup is very nice.'

Back outside I enjoy the combination of salty nuts and hoppy beer, and it's a pity the sun is no longer shining, but it's gone for the day now. I'll just have two pints here, then get a quick shower at Rydal Hall campsite and head back to camp. I ask myself if I really need a shower after swimming in the lake and decide that I want one anyway – partly to warm myself up because that dip in the cold water has left me shivery. I drink up, take the glass to the bar with a 'See you next time', get into the car and drive round to the campsite for a hot shower. And then it's back to camp, driving back through Ambleside and then taking the road to Hawkshead.

The Lone Wolf

This Hawkshead road is probably the worst road in the Lake District for irritating tourist traffic. Many visitors are fearful of the relative narrowness of the road that is bounded on both sides by stone walls. They drive very slowly and cautiously, often in the middle of the road, and are apt to suddenly come to a halt if they see a vehicle coming the other way, even though there's plenty of width for two cars. But you also get buses and coaches and timber waggons using this road, and they can really hold up the traffic. This evening though it's not too bad, and I can easily overtake the slow-moving car on the straight section between the junctions for Barngates and Wray. I carry on through Outgate, and then take a sharp left turn up a lane. This really is a narrow road and I have to proceed with care, lest someone is coming the other way, or there are lambs about, or maybe chickens or children up by High Loanthwaite Farm. I stop briefly at the farm to buy half a dozen free-range eggs from the porch, dropping my £1.50 in coins into the honesty box. Beyond the farm the lane bends round to the left and I'm driving up a single-track 'tunnel' bounded by high hedges and then woodland on both sides. At another bend in the lane there's a stony track on the left and an old National Trust metal sign saying 'PRIVATE ROAD' and I turn down here. The track winds through the trees, and after less than a hundred yards there's a pull-in area on the left under a big old oak tree. I reverse the car into here, beside the pile of gravel and I'm home, almost. From here there's a path leading into the wood, a path that I've made myself by all my comings and goings, a path that winds through the trees on dead twigs and grass and bare muddy earth in places. It drops down to the stream, where I can stride over a narrow bit. And then up the bank on the other side there's the small clearing and my camp.

I get that feeling of coming home, even though I've only been here a few weeks, and I'm only here temporarily. The first thing I do is to peg out my wet running shorts, shoes and towel on a washing line I've strung up between two small tree trunks – not that they'll dry very well now that the sun's gone down, but they can drip dry to some extent. The next thing to do is to get a fire going. It's getting chilly now and a fire provides some heat, obviously, as well as it being some 'company' and entertainment for the evening. I've got a stash of kindling twigs under the flysheet at the side of the storage tent, and stacked up on the grass is a small pile of sawn logs which I cut this morning. I start off by scrunching up some newspaper into loose ball shapes and lay these on the ash bed of the fireplace. The paper feels slightly damp to the touch, and I'm finding it almost impossible to keep things dry here, which is why I'm also going to put a couple of chunks of paraffin firelighter into the paper. I have lit fires here without using them, but fire-lighters can make it a whole lot easier and it means I shouldn't have to spend ages coaxing the fire into life and then watching over it all the time to make sure it's going. Next I put on some kindling and small logs, then light a corner of newspaper with my gas lighter. The damp paper doesn't burn very well, and I have to try again. When a flicker licks the firelighter a stronger flame arises and starts to work on the wigwam of kindling I've constructed. I have to watch over it for a while and blow on it gently to fan the flames into a little blaze. This first stage always looks promising as the newspaper goes up with a whoosh and a lot of heat is suddenly generated. But that initial whoosh soon dies down and now I have to nurse the fire by blowing on it and re-arranging the kindling sticks and logs to get it to that critical point where it has a life of its own with a strong red core and a healthy momentum of flame-vitality.

Now that I've got the fire going I need to get a meal together and the plan is to have an omelette with boiled potatoes and baked beans. The first thing to do is to get a kettle full of water on to boil on the big stove. I filled up all three of my litre water bottles at the campsite, so I've got plenty of water. I sometimes get my drinking water from the house, but I try to avoid going down there now, lest I get asked by Dorothy to do some job like scrubbing the shower floor or weeding the garden. The water in the nearby stream I only use for washing my hands and face. It's run through fields with cows and sheep before it gets

30

to the wood, so I certainly wouldn't trust it for drinking. In the storage tent I've got a bag of new potatoes and a tin of beans. Also I've got the eggs I just bought from the farm to make the omelette. I don't know much about foraging for wild food but I do know there is plenty of wild garlic, also known as ramsons, in the wood, a bit further down the track, so I set off with my scissors to harvest some of this to put in the omelette. And then I get cooking, which involves using the big stove on the wooden table and also my little backpacking stove, which I stand on a piece of slate on the ground.

As I'm waiting for the potatoes to boil I crack open a can of beer and sit in the chair for a while, watching the fire – which I suppose is an alternative to watching television. I also stare into the trees and see the movement of a deer in the distance. The daylight is fading, but the fire is roaring away nicely now. I get up to check on the spuds and then whisk up a couple of eggs in a mug with a fork. I transfer the pan of spuds to the small stove and put the frying pan on the big stove, with a little oil in it. And once the whisked eggs are in I add snipped up stems of the ramsons. As the omelette cooks I transfer the cooked potatoes onto my green plastic camping plate and pour two-thirds of the tin of baked beans into the pan, to heat up on the stove. And then finally I assemble my meal on the plate and sit down in the chair to eat. And it's good simple grub, much needed and appreciated after a day at work, followed by my run and swim. I have a good appetite and I eat a good amount, and then just sit there awhile, feeling satisfied.

It'd be nice to have some good company, someone with whom to talk about my day, but I don't need it and solitude is fine, possibly better. I can reflect on my day to myself and I don't need anyone else. I reflect on how I hate my job at the shop and wonder what else I could possibly do that would be more meaningful and satisfying. Perhaps a return to veggie catering, and perhaps a move out of the area at some point. I'd like to live more in a community, although at the same time I do value my privacy and solitude. But too much solitude is a bad thing and I do get lonely sometimes, it has to be said. I want for more friendship, some intelligent conversation, and *female* company, of course. But for the time being this is my life: the lone wolf living in the woods and going to work in the tourist town, where he feels little connection with the rest of humanity and no sense of community. The town is mainly just a market place, where people buy and sell, produce and consume. There are no values beyond getting and spending – except of course for playing in the outdoors. I could play all day every day, running and walking around the fells and swimming in the lakes, but ultimately it would get boring because I also need to do creative work, meaningful work, work in the context of a community of like minds, not slaving for some faceless corporate cash register. Is this possible? The light is fading in the wood. I drink a little beer and then put the radio on – the Marc Riley show on BBC Radio 6 Music. And I put the kettle on to heat up some water for washing up.

It's getting dark as I finish my pots, which I leave to drain on top of the big table. It's also getting cold, so I decide to retire to my sleeping tent, leaving my boots in the porch area, then getting undressed, putting on my thermals and getting under the duvet to read a little of *Green Man, The Archetype of our Oneness with the Earth* by William Anderson. It's a book I found yesterday in Ambleside library, and it seems to fit with my woodland-dwelling existence. The blurb on the jacket says: 'The Green Man, the perennial symbol of our unity with the natural world, the male image of our rootedness in the earth awakens from slumber as our civilization faces the prospect of ecological catastrophe.' It sounds promising, although at first there is a lot on church architecture and I find the style a bit dry. It was written in 1990, over twenty-five years ago, and I wonder if the author's ideas about the resurgence of the Green Man signifying 'a recovery of the sense of the sacred in Nature, and of a new humility among scientists' have proved to be over-optimistic as that 'ecological catastrophe' looms ever closer. The ideas are good though, and reflect a world view in tune with my own. On the last page of the book the author says in conclusion: *Our remote ancestors said to their mother Earth: 'We are yours.' Modern humanity has said to Nature: 'You are mine.' The Green Man has returned as the living face of the whole earth so that through his mouth we may say to the universe: 'We are one.'* Anyway, I'm tired now and can't get into a comfortable reading position so I put the book down, put my ear plugs in, turn off my headtorch and put my head down to sleep.

Breaking Free from the Leash

8.25am. Rain patters on the tarp, but a ray of sunlight beams through the trees to create a stripe of light on a trunk and a pool of light below the holly tree. Two robins flit between low branches and hop along the ground. One comes towards me, curious about my presence, it seems. That's robins for you – friendly birds who come close just to say 'hello' to you.

When I awoke this morning I thought about sex, as I so often do. There is something about camping in the wood that makes me feel horny. There is a sexual energy in the wood, an early summer vitality and sexuality given off by the multifarious flora and fauna that live here. The sweet smell of that honeysuckle alone is enough to turn me on. The woods were once a place where young people went to have sex – away from parents and siblings and crowded houses. The woods were a place of sexual freedom. My friend Ian Robinson tells me that one theory for the origin of his surname is that it means someone conceived in a wood, overlooked by a robin. And I've read in *Green Man* that traditionally on May Day, in this country and throughout many parts of peasant Europe, young people would go into a nearby wood after midnight, accompanied by music and the blowing of horns to play games and have sex and to break off branches of trees to adorn them with flowers. They would then take one of the branches, lop off its twigs, decorate it with purple bands and violets, then carry it to the village to erect it on the green or near the church – for maypole dancing.

Also when I awoke this morning I had a feeling of weight in my mind from knowing that Dorothy would be expecting me to go down to the house and make her a drink and whatever else. But I need to do my own thing here at camp first thing – get my breakfast, write in my journal, look around me, think, cut some firewood etc. It's difficult to relax when I know she's expecting me. The deal with her is that I give her some of my time in return for use of the house for showers, drinking water and the washing machine. She's already got two other helpers so she doesn't really need my help – it's just a matter of principle to her, an exchange so that I'm not getting something for nothing. But I've been thinking that what I get out of the deal isn't worth the trouble of doing the things she expects of me. She thinks I should give an hour a day which, as well as taking up the early morning drink may consist of making her a salad lunch, setting the fire, chopping logs, scrubbing the shower room floor or fetching something from town. When I take the cup of tea up to her room she has scraps of paper on which she's written lists of things for me to do, and there's always something else, something extra. 'Ooh,

and can you just do this, can you just do that...?' And
then she's often texting me, reminding me to do
things, or wondering where I am. Fortunately there
isn't usually a mobile signal in the wood. Anyway, she
told me earlier this morning when I went to see her
that she doesn't want me using the house anymore
because with her two live-in helpers there is too much
strain on the private water supply. I don't think there
is really, because I checked the water tank yesterday
and there was plenty in there. However, I am happy to
keep away from the house as I'm tired of getting
embroiled in doing all these little jobs for her. I've
already been taking showers at the campsites to keep
away from the house, I can get fresh drinking water
from the campsites too and I can do my laundry at the
launderette in Ambleside. So I feel a weight has been
lifted now. The wood doesn't belong to her anyway,
but to the National Trust, of which she's a tenant. She
doesn't mind me staying in the wood until such time
as I find a room, although I'll have to be as discreet as
possible as I'm sure the National Trust wouldn't like
me being here, if they knew. Fortunately Dorothy says
that they rarely venture into the wood as they would
have no reason to do so. It's not a managed wood, and
there's no public right of access since it belongs with
the house.

A few years ago I camped on some National Trust
land in Grasmere. I was working temporarily at the
Butharlyp How youth hostel, but I found the live-in
accommodation intolerably noisy from the big groups
of kids and the constantly slamming doors. So I
decided to pitch my old Lichfield ridge tent on the

wooded knoll at the back of the hostel as a place to get a more peaceful night's sleep. I walked up there after one evening's shift to find the tent had gone. It was quite a shock. Someone had stolen it! There was an expensive down sleeping bag and Thermarest in there too. Who would have taken it? I suspected that it might be the Trust. Of course you're not supposed to pitch up on 'their' land, and there may even be a sign near the bottom saying 'NO CAMPING'. Also it's a popular place with local dog-walkers and some busy-body could've informed them. So I called in at their nearby office to ask if they'd taken it, and yes indeed they had and it was being kept at their depot up at Red Bank. When I went to collect it there was no apology. They said they thought it had been 'abandoned', complete with sleeping bag and mat. You'd think they might have at least left a note to say they'd taken it. After all, it could've been my only home. But no, that's not how the National Trust operate.

And so I have to be careful not to advertise my presence here in the wood. My tents and tarp are green and can't be seen from the track or the lane, but if I hang up something brightly-coloured on the washing line it could flag up my being here. Also smoke from the fire in the evening could give me away, although National Trust rangers don't generally work in the evenings, besides which the smoke dissipates to some extent in the trees and it could be difficult for someone on the lane to pinpoint where it was coming from. And anyway, the wood is attached to the house, the tenant of which is allowed to use it, and she's permitting me to use it, which I think makes it something of a grey area. I don't know how long I'm going to be here. It could be just a few weeks, or it might be all summer. Although it's not an easy way to live I actually feel privileged to live like this because it's not the sort of thing that is usually possible in the Lake District. You can wild camp up in the fells, and I've plenty of experience of that, but camping in woods – which are a more natural place to camp, certainly for long-term camping – is generally out of the question, except perhaps for one or two nights of 'stealth' camping, because the woods are all owned and often patrolled by rangers, dog-walkers and others who don't like to see people camping in non-designated places.

Talking of dog-walkers I hear the slam of a car door on the lane, then the constant yapping and yelping of a little dog – a dog being taken for a walk by its 'owner' in the wood on the other side of the lane, no doubt. Why do people have to have a four-legged friend to justify going for a walk? The excitable little thing keeps yapping and yelping away, even though it must be off the leash and running about the freedom of the wood now. Maybe it's yelping for joy, but it's a very annoying noise. Why do people have to have 'pets' anyway? Personally I've never felt the desire or need to have a pet dog or cat or whatever. It's not that I don't like animals, just that I'd rather see them wild, rather than domesticated. This whole domestication of animals culture is very questionable, if you ask me. Having a pet dog is all about owning something, a furry living consumer accessory that can be *controlled.* All you have to do is feed them and walk them and they will be loyal to you, but they will have lost their dignity. They become your slave and you are the master. This is the relationship that pet owners want – having control, mastery over another living thing. The dog is trained, mastered, controlled, and quite often has its balls cut off so that it becomes more manageable, easier to tame, to subdue and control. A lot of dog owners prefer their relationships to their dogs than to their partners or friends or other humans because they are easier. Dogs don't answer back. You can stroke them and cuddle them and even treat them as surrogate children. Human relationships are complicated and troublesome, but the canine relationship is simple. Just feed and walk the thing and it will show you 'love'. And of course people love their dogs in return.

The relationship that some parents have with their children is similar to pet ownership. Their kids, like their dogs, are possessions, ego-extensions that they can control, train, manage and try to mould into their likeness. As the kids grow older they may feel themselves to be prisoners within the oppressive walls of nuclear family domestication. They may rebel and long to fly the nest and make their own way, or they might honour their captors without asking too many questions because they know on which side their bread is buttered.

Animals are domesticated, humans are domestic-ated. We live in a tame world where nearly everyone and everything is tamed and controlled, a world of masters and servants or slaves, a world where the slaves quite often don't see themselves as such, and where the masters often don't realise quite how controlling they are. I prefer to see wild animals and wild humans. To be a wild human is tricky in this society. If you are too wild you will end up on the wrong side of the law. But just to be an independent thinker is a good start. Whilst it's true that many manacles are self-made, it's also true that many are imposed on us by conditioning, the education system, our upbringing. If we can break free from at least some of those societal manacles of civilisation and domestication, if we can break free from the leash and run wild in the woods or the fells for a while then it will be good for the soul, for our vitality and dignity as a human being. And we might start to see the world in a different way, a wilder way or a more poetic way, and find a deeper connection with Nature that may actually help us to be useful members of society.

I've got half an hour before I set off to work in the shop. I put the kettle on for another coffee and set off into the trees to go for my morning shit. On the way back I snap off some dead hazel poles and take them for kindling. And then I collect a load of dead leaves, which I put into a big plastic container, and which I then sprinkle onto the path between the camp and the track to help bind the mud. I spend about ten minutes doing this, then saw a few logs, and then it's time to head into town.

Getting and Spending

It takes about fifteen minutes to drive into Ambleside, and I park up in one of the two designated shop parking spaces. Next to it is a skip full of old furniture and carpet from the Queens Hotel and I have a quick look, thinking some of the carpet would be useful for the camp, but I'll have to come back in my lunch break for a proper look as I don't want to be late for work, even though I don't really want to be there. And so I walk round to the shop, with my rucksack and plastic carrier bag containing my three litre water bottles.

Sharon goes through the shop targets and objectives for the day, one of which is to complete the processing of the delivery we didn't finish yesterday. And so begins another day in the shop. I spend the morning working with Paul on the delivery, putting price stickers on the hang cards, putting security tags on, and hanging it all up on a rail beside the till. The awful muzak goes on and on. It's a beautiful sunny day outside and I feel trapped in a place I don't want to be. I serve some customers, which is the best bit, although I don't feel good about selling them crap. Some of them know that our stuff is not good quality, but they don't want to spend much. Sometimes they have completely unrealistic expectations such as wanting a pair of waterproof boots that will take them safely up and down Scafell Pike, but they don't want to spend more than £30. One customer comes in to return a pair of £50 walking boots that are falling apart after only a few weeks. Another customer comes in and says she always buys from our shop because she knows it's 'good quality'. She has a branch in her home town in the Midlands, where it's probably the only 'outdoor' shop and so she's been easily converted into being a brand-loyal customer.

At 2pm I take my half-hour lunch break. I get my usual cheese roll from The Picnic Box, then walk up the hill to the bench, where I sit in the sun to eat and watch passers-by, one of whom is a lad from one of the other outdoor shops – where I worked for a season a few years ago. It's an independent, and probably the best outdoor shop in town to work at, but even there I found the work soul-destroying for much of the time. It was just another prison. The sun would be shining outside, but I was denied it. Eight hours a day of standing around (no hands in pockets, no leaning on stands), waiting for customers, tidying rails, moving stock around for no good reason, polishing mirrors that didn't need polishing – just to be seen to be busy doing *some*thing, then approaching customers, asking them if they needed any help. Some of them wanted advice, and some wanted to chat about where they were going walking, but many wanted to be left alone to browse, to fondle the latest technical fabric, to check the price tags, to go and compare with what was on offer at all the other outdoor shops just a short walk away, or go home and do the actual buying online. And at 5.30pm I would feel drained by the meaninglessness of it all.

What is life? Doing a job you don't really want to do, exchanging forty-odd hours a week of your time for a paltry wage that enables you to just about survive – to pay your rent and to put food on your plate and beer in your glass, and petrol in your car so that you can commute to said job? Of course you have your free time to recover – to play in the outdoors and blow your mind and tire out your body and re-claim your soul – before it's back to the stupid meaningless spirit-sapping treadmill again. You can do it for so long. Some people manage to do it all their lives. Some switch shops every now and again for a change of scene, but it's pretty much the same thing wherever you go. And it's not why you moved to the Lake District in the first place, but you have to survive and what else are you to do? It's either this or catering. Anyway, I got sick of it all, the same tired old loop, and so I moved out of the area, which I may do again in the autumn.

I have a moment to sit peacefully and reflect before I get up and go back down the hill to the shop. But I've still got five minutes left so I go and have a look in the skip next to the Queens Hotel and pull out a couple of rolls of carpet, one red and one blue, and I manage to get these into the car. It looks like new carpet – off-cuts perhaps from an ongoing refurbishment project. And then it's back into the courtyard of shops, where tourists wobble around in their lifestyle clothing, eating ice-creams. In one corner a number of staff are gathered for a smoke break. They're not all from the same shop, but they know each other and are mostly students. One of them is Sharon. In a shop window on the other side of the courtyard a clothing shop has a poster in the window advertising for part-time staff. It starts with the words: 'ARE YOU PASSIONATE ABOUT RETAIL?'

Who is truly passionate about retail? If this is someone's 'passion' there must be something wrong with them is all I can say. Selling 'lifestyle' leisure wear to tourists in return for the minimum (non-living) wage is surely not something that any real human being could be expected to be *passionate* about. It's just a job, of course, but these days people are expected to join in with spouting all sorts of insincere nonsense about their 'careers'. Oh yes, I'm absolutely passionate about selling checked shirts and chino trousers to bored and directionless anonymous random punters who are drifting around the shops looking to spend money on something, anything to give some kind of meaning, some sense of gratification in their lives. If shopping is the number one pastime in this country, perhaps some people might say that they are 'passionate' about shopping, just as they are passionate about their jobs which provide them with the wherewithal to do the shopping. Passionate about 'getting and spending'? What kind of a society is this?

Getting and spending, we lay waste our powers; / Little we see in Nature that is ours; / We have given our hearts away, a sordid boon! The poet William

Wordsworth wrote these lines as part of his sonnet 'The World Is Too Much With Us around 1802, attacking society's obsession with time and money and the accumulation of material goods, at the same time losing touch with Nature and thus selling their souls. That was over two hundred years ago, and since then things have got much worse. Romanticism has been discredited in some university English departments, in favour of an anti-Nature postmodernism. The Lake District, at one time a retreat from the getting and spending materialism and consumerism of the towns and cities, a place to come and commune with Nature for spiritual refreshment, has become just another place to spend money and consume stuff. If only Wordsworth could see Ambleside today...

'Are you passionate about retail?' Of course the word 'passionate' is much over-used nowadays. People claim all sorts of humdrum things to be their passion, but the word 'passion' is really not about everyday things. It infers heightened emotion, *intense* and barely controllable love or anger. One dictionary definition of passion is 'strong enthusiasm', and the root of enthusiasm is from the Greek *enthusiasmos*, from *entheos*, 'possessed by a god, inspired', and enthusiasm used to refer to strong *religious* emotion. So the words 'passionate' and 'enthusiastic' have become devalued in modern society, where people use these adjectives to describe their liking of their wage-slavery or of football or of wine or chocolate or some commonplace activity or object to consume.

Life itself has become devalued in modern, and especially *urban* society – an artificial society that lacks true enthusiasm or passion, these having been replaced by a culture of getting and spending in which the god is *money*. Life is controlled by governments, employers, banks, shopkeepers. The Western civilised way has long since lost its way, or rather gone so far down a dead-end road it is heading for an inevitable crash. We may take inspiration from history or from surviving indigenous peoples around the world, but the Western way dominates the entire globe to such an extent that we are all surely doomed.

And yet we are still alive. *I* am still alive. We may not be able to save our world now, but I can do what I can to go on living – not just surviving on the endgame treadmill of quiet desperation, but trying to live abundantly, enthusiastically, *passionately*. From where shall I draw inspiration? Not from the town or the television or the internet or my job, but from Nature, *wild* Nature, the wilder the better, for it is in wild Nature that I can re-wild my own nature and be the most alive and free.

But for the time being I'm stuck in the shop, processing the delivery – putting price stickers on the hang cards, putting security tags on and hanging it all up on a rail beside the till. The awful muzak goes on and on. Outside it's a beautiful sunny day and I wish I was on the fells. Around 4pm I volunteer to take the flat-packed cardboard from the delivery boxes down to the recycling bins. I just want to get out of the shop for a break, get a bit of sunshine on my face and some fresh air. It takes two trips with a load under each arm, and it's a walk of about a hundred yards down Compston Road, past more outdoor shops and a coffee shop, a struggle to get past the slowly-walking tourists and their dogs on tripwire leads, people walking along with their heads down, staring at their smartphones, clutching cardboard cups of coffee, a sea of slowly-moving people wearing outdoor or lifestyle clothing, drifting with the tide, moving in waves in and out of the outdoor shops and the coffee shops. The traffic is slow-moving up the road and the air is full of petrol and diesel fumes. I turn left at the coffee shop up The Slack and take the cardboard to the recycling area, where I throw it in a large wheelie bin. And then I walk back up the road, calling in briefly to say hello to Steve B-M at Fred Holdsworth's Bookshop – an island of intelligence and culture in a sea of dumbed-down consumerism.

Back in 'my' shop there isn't much time to go now before I knock off and drive back towards Hawkshead, to go to work at the pub. I put out some delivery, serve a few customers, then clock out at 5pm, fill my water bottles and say 'See you'. I start work at the pub at 6pm, so there'll be enough time to call back at the wood and drop off those rolls of carpet.

Outside the Gate

At the wood I park up under the oak tree and pull the rolls of carpet out of the car. There's a long narrowish blue piece and a large square red piece. The red piece is quite heavy and awkward to carry, but I take them one at a time to the camp, where I lay the red piece below the tarp – my 'living room' carpet, and roll out the blue piece beside it, towards the storage tent. When I first set up camp here the ground was carpeted in grass and bluebells, but with all my walking around, and all the wet weather we've had lately, the ground has become increasingly muddy, and so the idea is to create a barrier against the mud. The carpet is nice and thick and seems to be of good quality. The colours are rather bright, and that goes against my efforts to keep discrete, but then again they brighten the place up and lend a happy, hippy vibe to my woodland home. I walk back to the track to see from there how visible they are and yes, they do show up a bit, but perhaps only when you know where to look. And I guess they'll tone down in time, once they've been rained on and soiled by the mud.

Walking back into the wood I notice how the path I've made has become quite distinct now, and this also goes against my trying to stay discrete. At first I tried to walk in and out by slightly different routes, but now I usually just follow this path – although when I get closer to the beck the way becomes very wet and muddy. Dorothy came into the wood on her off-road buggy the other day – to see me, or at least to see where I'm camping. And she got herself grounded in this muddy area and had to phone the farmer at Loanthwaite to ask him to come and rescue her. She'd never have got over the stream and up the bank on the other side, even if she hadn't got stuck in the mud. Anyway, I've started crossing the stream at another point, where it's wider, but the approach is drier. The thing is, when there's been a lot of rain the stream here will be impassable without getting very wet feet, so I'm planning to lay down some stepping stones. As I look down at the stream I think I'd like to get started on that now, it being a nice dry and sunny evening, but unfortunately I've got to go and work at the pub. I stand there, listening to the peaceful sound of running water and birdsong for a while, but I really need to get down to the Outgate Inn, and it's a shame to be rushing around for so much of the time.

At the Outgate the first thing I do is to get myself a pint of Dizzy Blonde from smiling Jo at the bar. And then I sit outside on the bench at the front for five minutes, sunning my face and enjoying the beer. I look up at the pub sign, which depicts a fox looking at its cub by a five-bar wooden gate. The fox is *outside* the gate presumably, outside the gated community, the flock of sheep, society.

And then at 6pm it's into the kitchen, where I am greeted by Kat and Raz and a pile of washing up. Actually there's not too much washing up to start with as they've been keeping on top of it. But it's on with my rubber gloves to clear what there is, before things start to get busy. Kat tells me that she's made a veggie chilli with rice for my dinner, and so after just ten minutes of washing up I break off to have my meal with the rest of my pint in the back beer garden. And I have to say this is a good little job. The washing up itself may be tedious, but the people here are good, I can have a beer on the job and Kat provides me with a free meal. Can't be bad. I enjoy the chilli and rice and then return to the kitchen, where some orders have come on. And it's the usual sort of meaty fare of steak in ale pies, 'Lamb Henry', gammon, fish and chips etcetera, except that I think the quality here is certainly better than average. Presentation-wise they've followed the trend of serving meals on roofing slates and chips in little wire baskets, which I personally don't like, but perhaps this is what customers round here expect now. In the seventies it was chicken in the basket, but now it's chicken on a roofing slate. The world of catering seems bizarre sometimes. What's wrong with plates?

The sink is full of very hot soapy water, and as chef Raz cooks various things for the orders he uses lots of different pans and utensils, which have to be washed in the sink and then piled on top of the dish-washing machine to dry. And then the waiting-on staff for the evening, Zoe and Johnny, bring in empty plates and cutlery, which I wash in the machine. As the evening goes on the volume of washing up increases, and towards the end there are loads of greasy pots and pans to wash as Raz clears down his area. Last orders in the pub is at 8.00pm, which means I can usually get finished by about 9.30pm, and tonight is no exception. It's been a three-and-a-half-hour shift, which included a short dinner break, and then I have another pint at the bar before heading back to the wood in the car. It's dark outside now and it feels cold after the heat of the kitchen. I could do with a shower, but I don't feel like going round to one of the campsites at this hour, so it can wait 'til tomorrow.

Back at the wood I make my way through the trees by the light of a torch. And, although it's 10pm now, I decide to get a fire going as I don't want to go to bed just yet. I make myself a herbal tea, then I sit in the chair under the tarp and read the final pages of *Green Man* by the light of my headtorch and with a crackling fire for company. I put on a couple of beech logs and they hiss from the water content, but will burn slowly. *In tracing the story of the Green Man we saw how he first appeared at the end of one period of the experience of humanity, that of participation in Nature, a barely conscious union of the spirit with the world of vegetation. It was a world of deep kinship with trees and woods, to which people felt as close as to their own families and tribes. The Green Man then adapted to the changing attitude to Nature of the onlooker awareness brought about by the growth of western science and technology...* As I sit there reading, moths and crane flies fly into my face, attracted by the light of the headtorch. I wave them away with my hand, but it's distracting and annoying. I carry on regardless for a while, then switch off the lamp and just sit there watching the fire and thinking about the day. I switch the light back on, read a little more, then finally go to bed about midnight.

The Claim I've Staked

Waking to the sound of a woodpecker tapping tentatively at a trunk up above, I slept well last night, following my shift at the pub and then reading *Green Man*. It's a dry morning for a change, sunlight is streaming through the trees and the birds are singing more than usual. As I sit in my chair, having had my breakfast, the robin comes to greet me. He flits between low branches and the ground, watching me. Robins are like this everywhere, curious about humans, *friendly* it seems, or are they just hoping for food? I don't think it's a food thing because if it was they would come closer. They are like messengers from another dimension, although what the message is I don't know.

Today is a day off from the shop, it's going to be a fine sunny day and I want to go for a run on the fells. But there's no rush, and I want to spend some time just enjoying being in the wood and doing a bit of woodland path maintenance. I also need to spend some time filling in the potholes on the track with gravel – a job I promised Dorothy I'd do. But first I'll just drink my coffee and stare into the trees for a while. And as I sit quietly I see a reddish-brown roe deer just twenty yards away, inching along as it grazes the ground, bent right over, it's face to the living floor. I see it chewing a leaf, but it doesn't see me. I share the wood with a pair of these creatures, although I've only seen one lately. They are beautiful animals, but shy. They keep their distance – which is not surprising since they've been hunted down the centuries and still are by 'wildlife rangers' of the Forestry Commission at nearby Grizedale Forest. 'Grizedale' means valley of the wild boar, and wild boars were hunted to extinction in this country seven hundred years ago, although so-called 'wild boar burgers' (farmed really, of course) are sometimes on the menu at a local pub. Deer are not in danger of extinction, and the Forestry Commission say that their numbers are increasing and they are regarded as a pest (although also a useful resource to sell as meat) in their managed plantations. But here in the wild wood they do no harm. It's their natural habitat and I say 'live and let live'. We share this living space amicably. I respect them and wish them no harm. And they respect the claim I've staked on the wood and keep their distance – except for this morning, and as I watch this deer it's now just ten yards away, moving slowly forwards, head bent to the ground, still foraging for whatever it is it likes to eat. Muscular haunch, slender lower legs, cute face, beautiful red-brown coat of fur. It looks up, sees me and is shocked, its body suddenly tensing up as it takes fright and then flight – turning round and bounding off into the trees but staying within eyesight, watching me from a safe distance.

It's time to get moving and doing some practical tasks, and first I want to do a little maintenance work on my woodland path, which is getting very muddy in places. I get the big old plastic container that had been discarded for recycling, empty out the rainwater in the bottom and take it towards the holly tree, where I fill it with dead leaves and twigs. These holly leaves are tough and take a long time to rot down so they're good for my purpose. And then I walk from the camp to the track on the path, sprinkling the leaves and twigs onto the muddy patches as I go – to bind with the mud and effect a temporary repair. 'Erosion control' I suppose you could call it. But there are some very muddy areas that need more than just leaves and twigs, and so for these bits I dredge up some small stones from the beck with my shovel and sprinkle these onto the mud as well as the leaf litter. Whilst I'm doing this I realise that I might as well divert the path away from the very muddy area towards the wider section of the beck – with its little 'beach', where I'll have to lay down some stepping stones.

After this I walk down to the house to get the wheelbarrow and shovel. Fortunately nobody is about outside so I can just get on with it without being distracted. I wheel the barrow up the track towards the pile of gravel where I park my car, but on the way there I stop to look at a broken-down dry stone structure beside the track in the adjacent field. It was perhaps once a sheep shelter or small outhouse of some sort, but is now just a ruin. Anyway, there are some nice big pieces of stone here that I can use for my stepping stones, so I climb carefully over the barbed wire fence, select a few good ones, put them in the wheelbarrow and wheel them up the track to the gravel pile. Then I carry the five pieces one by one into the wood and down to the stream. I've got one more piece than I need, but I place the four best ones on the stream bed at roughly equal distance from each other. I use the shovel a bit to make sure they are securely bedded down in the silt and try walking on them. One piece has got a bit of a wobble, so I have to bed it down deeper and at a different angle, but then I'm finished and I'm pleased with my handiwork. It didn't take long, but now I've got a better way across the stream and built a bit more of myself into my woodland home.

Next I need to get on with filling the pot holes in the track. It's a job that the National Trust sometimes do, but they don't come very often and so we have to do it from time to time to keep on top of it. When there's been wet weather and vehicles go up and down the shallow hollows become deepened and are not good for cars, and especially not good for Dorothy in her buggy. And so I fill up the barrow with gravel and wheel it down the track, stopping now and then to fill the holes and compress the gravel down with my feet or bash it down with the back of the shovel. This takes a while and I'm eager to get it finished so I can get away into the fells. Where the track runs through the wood you can't see very far, but when the trees stop as the track approaches the house you get a sweeping view taking in Coniston Old Man, Wetherlam, Crinkle Crags, Black Fell, High Raise, Loughrigg, Helvellyn, the whole of the Fairfield Horseshoe, Red Screes,

Caudale Moor, Wansfell and Ill Bell – surely one of the most extensive fell panoramas in the whole of the Lake District. I could do a recce on the route of my big round, but I've done enough of that over the last few months and it'd be nice to do something different so today I think I'll head to Coniston and go round Wetherlam, Swirl How and the Old Man. And so, after I've finished work on the track and Dorothy comes out to thank me, I fill up my water bottle at the house and get my running gear together.

Rascal How

It's only a fifteen-minute drive over Hawkshead Hill to Coniston, where I park up the lane behind the Black Bull, put my fell shoes on, fasten up my bum bag and set off jogging up the rough track into the Coppermines Valley. After about four hundred yards another track branches off on the right and I go up here, which leads to a row of old miners' cottages, all but one of which is now a holiday cottage. I used to drive up here a couple of years ago and park at the flat area at the top, just before the cottages. And then I'd walk in to my wild campsite up in High Blue Quarry, halfway up the flank of Wetherlam in an area of fell called Rascal How. But before walking up the hill I'd get my meal together at the car, cooking on my camping stove on a handy flat-topped rock, then sitting down to eat in the camping chair whilst admiring the sublime mountain arena around me. I'd wash my pots in the beck and then walk up the zig-zags of the old slate quarry track, past the first quarry, then the middle one, and finally arriving at the top one, where I made my home for three weeks, sleeping in the old Lichfield tent, which I'd pitched on a small flat grassy area a little way in from the narrow quarry entrance. I built a ring of stones fireplace near to the tent and sometimes had fires, using wood from a dead tree at the back of the quarry which I sawed into logs. I also built a small dry stone wall at the quarry entrance to keep the sheep out. The wall had a narrow opening I could pass through, via a 'gate' made of two large flat pieces of slate. I also placed a couple of dead tree branches on top of the low wall to deter the sheep from trying to jump and clamber over it. I wanted to keep the sheep out because they would come in at all hours of the night or early morning and disturb me with their clattering about on the loose slates of the spoil heaps. They liked being in the quarry themselves – for the shelter, I suppose. There were quite a lot of their droppings on the grass, and I picked up quite a few ticks during my stay there.

It turned out to be not a very sheltered place to camp because when it got windy the wind blew towards the quarry and was funnelled through the narrow entrance and the tent would flap around a lot and I wouldn't be able to get to sleep. To start with the weather was dry and sunny and calm, and it was an awesome place to camp – hidden away, off the main walkers path up the fell and enclosed by all this rock. The back wall of the quarry was pretty much a vertical drop of about a hundred feet into a tumble of boulders, and it was an impressive backdrop. There was some evidence of where rock climbers had been, with a couple of bolts hammered into the rock. Looking the other way there was a great view of Coniston Old Man, and to the left of that, in the distance, was Kirkby Moor with its wind turbines, and then Morecambe Bay. I remember getting up in the middle of the night to go for a pee and looking south to the twinkling lights of Barrow-in-Furness, and beyond that to the lights of Morecambe and Lancaster on the other side of the bay. There was a clear sky, filled with twinkling stars too, and it felt like a pretty amazing place to be – seemingly as far away from the towns as from the stars.

Then there was another night which was very stormy, when the wind was a gusting gale and it was lashing with rain, everything was cloaked in thick cloud and I had a sleepless night with the tent fabric flapping like mad and the sound of the occasional boulder crashing down the back wall of the quarry. I lived there for three weeks, leaving my tent up every day and going out to work at the shop in Grizedale, sometimes in the car, and sometimes by bike. I'd started out by camping at Bowkerstead Farm in Grizedale when I started the job. Previously I'd been living in Kendal and been unemployed for quite a while so I had no money, it was too far to commute and camping was the only option. The site at Bowkerstead was a good one, but when it got busy with the start of the school holidays I decided I'd rather camp wild. I also wanted to get out of the forest, where I felt hemmed in by trees and irritated by midges. I wanted to be in the wide open spaces of the fells. The Coniston fells were relatively handy so I did some exploratory walks, came across High Blue Quarry, and decided to just stay there.

I got a colleague friend at Grizedale to paint in her artistic hand the words 'Rascal How' on a piece of slate that I got from the quarry, and I propped this against a rock at the entrance for my own amusement, as if it was the name of a house on a street. But in the end I was driven out of the quarry by the stormy weather and too many sleepless nights. After about six weeks in the job at Grizedale I managed to scrape together enough money to move into a small flat at Kirkby-in-Furness, which was a fair commute from Grizedale, but which was the closest suitable and affordable accommodation I could find. But this turned out to be quite a short-lived address for me, as I found the flat cramped, claustrophobic and noisy from the family who lived upstairs. After camping out in the wilds with no neighbours I felt hemmed in by the walls of domestication, irritated by creaking floorboards and toilet noises from above, and I even got a bad back from the soft mattress, having been used to sleeping on just a thin foam mat in the tent. It was nice to have a kitchen, and useful to have somewhere to store all my stuff, but I couldn't relax there, and I resented having to pay a load of rent for what was essentially a noisy cramped box. So then I managed to find lodgings in Grizedale at a house with a woman who worked for the Forestry Commission, but that turned out to be an unhappy chapter as well.

Anyway, as I set off jogging up the zig-zags of the quarry track today, the memories of my time camping at Rascal How come back to me. Over there in the stream, in the shade under the little bridge was my 'beer fridge'. I would sit and sunbathe in the chair by the car and have a couple of beers before getting my evening meal. And then after my meal I'd walk up this track back to camp – and trust that the tent would still be there. From here the fence posts along the top rim of High Blue Quarry are just visible on the skyline. It takes about fifteen minutes to get there following this track, although on my first night, when I got here late and the light was fading, I took a direct line straight up the steep fellside, following the course of a stream to start with. That was an arduous route, especially with a heavy rucksack, and not to be repeated. But this quarry track is well-graded and makes for a pleasant walk, gradually gaining height as it switches back and forth. There are a lot of sheep droppings on the path today, and there are a lot of sheep about, but on that first night I came here there were virtually none, which seemed strange, until I realised they must have been herded down to the farm for shearing. The next day I called at the big campsite in Coniston to get a shower and the air was full of a horrible acrid smell and there were clouds of black smoke billowing from the neighbouring farmyard. And then I realised that they were burning the sheep fleeces. It's a shame that farmers do this, but if the fleeces are of no economic value it's understandable. The whole sheep farming industry in the Lakes makes no sense economically and only carries on with the help of government subsidies. The purpose of keeping it going seems to be because it's traditional, and of course because it's good for the tourist economy. When the tourists come they want to see their Lake District frozen in time, with the fells neatly manicured by grazing Herdwicks.

Walking past the first quarry I look in at the gorge-like entrance to the shady amphitheatre with its tumbled rocks and thick grass – and there are quite a few sheep in there, enjoying the shade and the juicy grass. When I came back to camp on my second evening the farmer and his dogs were returning the sheep to the fell, and the sheep looked odd with their new harsh haircuts, their dignity removed along with their wool. They were like a bunch of skin-headed prisoners being released back to the freedom of their fell – to join the few wild and woolly ones who'd evaded the round-up.

Onwards I trot along this track that leads to a rocky noddle in the distance. This outcrop is a great viewpoint overlooking the village and lake, and I feel drawn towards it, but have to remember to take a hard left turn on the switchback track that leads through walls of bracken and takes me towards the middle quarry. The Coniston Fell Race route goes this way and then skirts the bottom of the quarry to join up with the Mouldry Bank path up Wetherlam. But I'm going to take the path that leads to the top of this quarry, the path that skirts the very rim at the top, and where I have to take care because there's been a small landslip below a couple of trees hanging onto the edge, and after a bit of a ledge it's a sheer drop down. When I brought my friend Rob Sparkes with me this way one evening to show him my camp he remarked with a smile that this steep dangerous bit was a 'deterrent' to anyone walking this way. From here the grass path becomes rockier and is strengthened by pieces of slate set in the vertical plane. There's an old stone hut on the left that I looked at as a possible shelter, but the floor was carpeted in sheep shit, and also a dead sheep.

Suddenly the path levels out onto a broadish flat area, and there's the entrance to 'my' quarry. My wall has already broken down a bit, and as I walk through to the patch where I camped I see my fireplace stones have been dismantled – perhaps by a Park ranger wanting to destroy the evidence so as to discourage others from doing the same thing. You're not supposed to light fires in the fells, don't you know - it's against the Country Code or whatever. One evening I had a fire here and I was disturbed by a group of four walkers. It was a beautiful sunny evening and I was enjoying my solitude, cooking a meal and listening to the radio, when suddenly I heard voices and saw some figures looking down at me from the fence at the top of the back wall. A few minutes later they appeared at the quarry entrance. They said they were looking for a waterfall somewhere higher up the fell and were now on their way back down to Coniston. I don't know if they'd intended to drop down by the quarry, but they said they could smell my wood smoke from some distance away and were maybe drawn here by it. They were friendly enough and seemed impressed by my camp, especially when I told them that I went out to work in Grizedale. But one of the women said I shouldn't have fires and that she worked for the National Park but that she'd turn a blind eye to this one. It was like I was being cautioned by a police officer, although we all knew I wasn't doing any harm. I was hardly going to set the whole fell on fire, but rules are rules and all that. The wood I used was from a dead tree at the back of the quarry that I'd sawn up that afternoon, it having been a day off. It was quite an adventure scrambling over the jumble of boulders to get to the tree with my saw and it felt like I was some kind of survivalist in the wilderness, rising to the challenge and relishing it. The back wall of the quarry in bright sunlight was an amazing sight: all the faces and edges of cloven rock at different angles, together making a sort of massive abstract painting, or maybe the subject for a painting by Julian Heaton-Cooper.

The flat patch of grass where I pitched my tent is now strewn with rocks and sprinkled with sheep droppings. Over to one side, near the spoil heaps, is the tree where a bird would sing every morning, waking me sometimes earlier than I would have wanted, but with a noise much more pleasant than any alarm clock. I turn and walk out of the quarry onto the big flat grassy area, and I've got a great view of Coniston Old Man. The quarry entrance faces directly west – towards the prevailing wind, so not the best orientation for shelter. Up to the right of the quarry there's a small stream, which is where I'd get my drinking water. As for going to the toilet, it wasn't as easy as in the wood in terms of burial, but I would walk past the ruined hut to the end of the flat area and make a hole as best I could in the rocky spoil at the end. Nearby is my 'lookout tower', a structure that once held the top end of the aerial ropeway that transported slate from the quarry to the valley. I climb up the steps to the top and it's a useful vantage point, that extra bit of height affording a view of the valley bottom, with the youth hostel at the end and the row of old miners' cottages directly below. Beside the tower is a section of rusty old iron cable, frayed at the edges – a remnant of the old ropeway I guess. There are lots of old structures and and bits and pieces of the quarrying industry lying around. Also there are a few 'sculptures', where people have used slate to make their personal mark on this post-industrial fellscape. There's one example just down there near the path – a sort of cairn that's hollow inside, like a shelter for a dog or some other animal.

I would build a stone shelter for myself up here – a hut complete with fireplace – to *live* up here, but of course that's not possible. The whole fell will be owned by someone so I'd have to buy the fell, and even then it would be against the planning regulations or whatever. The pioneering days are long gone, and yet it remains a romantic idea.

At one time – up until the early 1800s – it was permissible to build your own home anywhere on Dartmoor, as long as you could get four walls up, a roof on and a peat fire lit in the hearth within a single day. And there are lived-in homes on the moor today that started off as being self-built in a day. I wonder how far back in history you would have to go in the Lake District to a time when it was possible to simply build your abode in a place that took your fancy, without having to buy the land or ask for anyone's permission.

The Bit Between My Teeth

Anyway, I'm going to carry on with my run now, or rather *walk* initially as I head up the steep slope to the left side of the quarry. The sun is shining high in the sky and I'm feeling good in myself as I power walk up the steep slope, my body saying 'yes' to the physical challenge. The slope flattens out into an open grassy area, with rock outcrops here and there. I break into a run and wend my way through the undulations and crags, climbing a little at first, then dropping down into the high valley of Hole Rake, then continuing up the broad ridge of Wetherlam – and it always feels a bit of a drag going up here. There is the well-trodden main path, but also various minor paths that contour this way and that, looking for the best line up the fell. In the Coniston Fell Race runners take different routes, some confident to make their own way on reccied lines, but most happy to follow the pack following the main path. I remember doing the race over twenty years ago in '91 and getting a good contouring line to the right of the main path, and then when I joined the path higher up I'd gained quite a few places and caught up with my old mate Martin Davies. I was feeling strong that day and went on to get a good time and position – 1.16.39, 7th. Today I have to work hard at this climb, but my legs have got plenty of fell miles training in them and I've got the bit between my teeth.

Higher up, the ridge flattens out before the final climb to the top of Wetherlam. And from here the route gets a bit more inspiring, with the drop down to Swirl Hause and then the scramble up to Swirl How. On this scramble up the Prison Band I have to use my hands to haul myself up in places, and it adds a bit of 'spice' to the run. I remember when I was training for the race in '91 coming up here on my own one afternoon and surprising myself at how fit and strong I felt and how fluidly I navigated the climb, managing to keep running for most of the way. I'm not as fit and agile as I was then, but I'm feeling pretty good as I make my way upwards, enjoying the feel of the warm rock in my hands and the feel of being a wild animal moving confidently through the fell-world.

From the top of Swirl How it's an easy run, dropping down to Levers Hause to the right of the main path on a slanting line, and then the pull up to Brim Fell and up to the Old Man, where there are lots of people gathered round the huge summit cairn. I guess this must be one of the most popular fells to climb in the Lake District. I know of one man who walks up here every single day. I don't know if he takes the same route every time, but it seems rather unimaginative when there are plenty of other good fells around here. It is said that the Old Man is some sort of sacred mountain, a 'great spiritual power battery' charged with cosmic intelligence, so perhaps this could account for his fixation. There have been UFO sightings here over the years, and just the other week a customer came into the shop and said that the chip in her bank card had ceased to work since she walked up and down the Old Man.

Anyway, I don't linger at the summit and plunge down the steep slatey path that zig-zags down to Low Water – in places taking a very steep direct line that cuts through the zig-zags, and leaning back a little so that I don't fall head over heels. Lower down, at a switch back, I take a faint grassy trod that cuts a big corner and cuts out the bouldery path to the tarn, rejoining the main path that takes me down past the disused quarry workings – the ruins of stone huts, spoil heaps and rusty iron cables. At one point a cable crosses the path and it was here in the race that I swooped past Martin and managed to keep up a fast pace on the fiddly rocky path down to the Miners Bridge and then back down the main track to the finish field behind the village institute. Today I keep up a good pace too, but I'm not going to go flat out and risk turning an ankle or catching my toe on a rock and falling flat on my face. I have to concentrate and be nimble on my feet, constantly looking ahead for rock obstacles, no step the same – little steps, strides, jumps, twists and turns and keeping the forwards and downwards momentum, sometimes on the rocky path, sometimes veering off into the bracken for a faster line, down to a gate through a stone wall, then down to Church Beck and the Miners Bridge, where I stop to look down into the ravine towards the place where I used to bathe that summer I was camping at Rascal How. I decide to go and have a closer look, so I turn left over the bridge, walk a little way up the track and then clamber down the steep bank.

Sitting on a rock beside my bathing pool, it's a beautiful spot, the crystal-clear water enclosed by big clean boulders and overlooked by a rowan tree. A small waterfall plunges into the back of the pool, constantly refreshing the water. I would come here after a day's work at Grizedale, strip off and wash myself, putting my soap on a rock shelf beside the pool. Although the water was very cold, it left me feeling invigorated afterwards – more so than having a hot shower at a campsite. I'd have to keep an eye out for walkers on the path as I stripped off and then got dressed after my dip, but if they did happen to see me naked I wasn't really bothered.

Today, as I look around me, I see a beautiful little five-petalled pink flower growing out of a crevice in a rock. You don't get grazing sheep down here, and these gorges are good sanctuaries for all sorts of plant life you wouldn't see on the fells (although the many parties of ghyll-scrambling kids that come here might be a threat). Also sticking out of a rock is the stump of a rusty old iron rod, a remnant of some structure from earlier times and a reminder of man's industrial stake in wild Nature. This rod is literally a stake, a stake driven into the body of Mother Nature, a brutal penetration effected for some temporary utilitarian purpose that is now redundant. I climb back up the bank, then follow the main track down to the lane to where my car is parked. I drink some water, eat a dried fruit bar, get changed and then walk into the village and up the lane to the Sun Hotel.

At the bar I get myself a pint of Loweswater Gold, then go out to sit in the beer garden, the afternoon sunshine on my face. It's a nice peaceful spot, on the edge of the village, although it can get very busy during the summer. When I was camping at the quarry I'd sometimes come here or to the Black Bull for a couple of pints, but I'd usually feel irritated by the crowds of visitors and be glad to get back to my lair in the fells. I like drinking real ale but I only like pubs when they aren't busy, which isn't very often round here. This afternoon though it's quiet, with just a few others in the garden. From where I'm sitting there's a view up Coppermines Valley and I can see some of the fell skyline from whence I came, and to which I will no doubt return again.

I just have the one pint and then walk back to the car, via a visit to the Co-op for some fresh veg. I'd like to make a nice meal tonight, since I've got more time than usual. I'll make some sort of veg stew to have with rice, and so I buy a red onion, courgette, yellow pepper and a tin of chopped tomatoes, as well as some bottles of beer. And then I drive back over the hill, back home to my camp.

A Simple Sensual Pleasure

Back in the wood now it's only 4.00pm, and at this time of day quite a lot of sunshine gets into the clearing. I decide to light a fire, even though the air is still warm, and then just sit in the chair and relax with a couple of beers. The fire smokes a lot at first, and stings my eyes as I coax it to life. Then, as I sit back to watch, the smoke picks out a hundred laser-like sunbeams coming through the gaps in the green canopy – strands of solar light-energy that have travelled millions of miles from their fireball source. Fire is linked with fire – the fire in the hearth to the fire in the sky. I run to the car to get my camera, but when I get back the magical effect has gone. My fire has become less smoky and the fireball in the sky is now obscured by a small cloud. Everything is fleeting. We have to make the most of the here and now.

Settling back down in my chair I read some of the *Green Man* book: *It was a world of deep kinship with trees and woods, to which people felt as close as to their own families or tribes.* As I sit there reading I'm aware of a 'crack, crack' noise coming from somewhere inside the wood. It sounds a bit like someone chopping logs. I carry on reading: *In the Dark Ages we saw the Christian missionaries leading the attack on tree worship and thereby bringing about the psychic revolution in the attitudes to Nature from which Western science and technology sprang.* Again that 'crack, crack' noise. I decide to get up to go and investigate, walking in the general direction the sound is coming from, but I can't see anybody and the noise has stopped now. I wonder if it might be a tree coming down. Anyway, I return to my book and my beer.

By and by it's time to get some dinner on, and as someone who enjoys cooking I find that one of the main drawbacks of the camping life is not having a kitchen. Cooking with just one-ring camping stoves is a bit limiting, to say the least. However, with a bit of organisation it's still possible to make nice meals. I start by putting a pan of rice on to boil, and then I set to chopping up the veg, using my trusty old Sabatier six-inch knife and a wooden board. I do this chopping sitting down, with the board in my lap, since the table is piled high with all sorts of things: the veg, pans, plastic crockery, water bottles, beer bottles, notebook and radio. I put the radio on because music is a good accompaniment to cooking, whether in a kitchen or in the middle of a wood. Once the rice starts to boil I switch the pan to my little backpacking stove, which sits on a piece of slate on the ground, and start to fry the veg in a bigger pan on the bigger stove. And as the veg sautés in olive oil, releasing delicious aromas, I drink some beer and listen to the music on the radio. It would be nice to have someone to cook for or with, some *one*, or maybe a little tribe of us dwelling in the wood. Then again I am used to my own company, and maybe it's better this way most of the time.

I open a tin of beans, pour most of them into the stew and give it all a good stir. Once the rice is cooked I stir in some tamari soy sauce, and then splash a bit into the stew as well. I've discovered that salt doesn't keep well at the camp. It's too damp an environment and it soon clumps together and becomes difficult to use. So I tend to use soy sauce instead, as a sort of liquid salt. I also grind a good amount of black pepper into the stew, and then that's ready too and I'm ready to eat. I've got a healthy appetite after the day's fell-running and hardly any lunch, so the food goes down very well. A simple meal and a simple sensual pleasure, the enjoyment no doubt enhanced by being out of doors on a nice sunny evening with my wood fire burning and smoking away and some good tunes on Radio 6 Music. I feel I should learn how to cook on the open fire, and maybe I will when I get round to it, but I don't really want to make life more difficult for myself than it already is. To cook on the fire I could only use one pot and I'd have to rig up some sort of tripod and the fire would have to have been going for a good while, with plenty of glowing embers. And at the end of the day I'm not living like this for a 'bushcraft' holiday before I go back home to my house – because I don't have a house, and this is my only home.

After my dinner I just sit for a while, watching the fire and listening to the radio. I could get used to this. I like living close to Nature, although of course it's one thing in the summer and something else in the winter. Maybe I'll get sorted out with a room soon, although I like having my own space that's not confined by bricks and mortar, but gently enveloped by Nature's greenery: A ceiling of beech leaves, a couple of mossy trunks, no walls or doors ('unscrew the doors themselves from their jambs!'), an openness to the world, not cloistered in a box and alienated from Nature, but a part of Nature, an inseparable part of it. It could get lonely, and I wish I had friends, a community with whom to live like this. Whatever happened to the 'new age travellers'? Hounded by the authorities, driven back into towns and jobs and conventional grey law-abiding, mortgage/rent and council tax-paying citizenship. The government does not like travellers, nomads, freedom-seekers. We are all expected to be hard-working drones by day, and then safely locked up in our suburban cells by nightfall. But I'm not a new age traveller or a nomad; I'm a worker with a job, but with nowhere to live – no building that has a lockable front door and all the usual elements that make up what is considered to be a proper 'home' – plumbing, electricity, central heating, television etc. I am homeless really, in the usual sense, although being outdoorsy and a bit of a philosopher I am putting a positive spin on it.

I feel comfortable in this wood – comfortable in the knowledge that I'm not likely to get disturbed here because other people rarely come here. It feels private, and it *is* private, even though it isn't really mine. Also it's not as midgey as I thought it would be. Sometimes I wish I had more of a view, but I only have to walk a couple of hundred yards down the track for that. It feels secluded and secure and I can relax here, but the outside world isn't far away. The lane is only fifty yards away through the trees, and I can see people and vehicles (not that there are many) going up and down, although they can't see me. I've looked into the wood from the lane and it's difficult to see the camp. There's just one spot, if you know exactly where to look, where you can see a bit of it, although it's not obvious what it is. The village of Hawkshead is just about a mile away over the fields, and sometimes I hear noise from there, especially at the weekends – when there's live music at the pubs or wedding receptions or whatever. Sometimes I wear ear plugs at night and sometimes I don't. It seems a shame to wear them, but I don't want to get disturbed by a vehicle on the lane, or by music from the village, or even the nocturnal noises of wildlife in the wood. Quite often when I turn off my torch to settle down to sleep I hear a rustling through the dead leaves beside the tent. It sounds like it could be a mouse or something like that, but I've come to the conclusion that it could be something as small as a beetle. It wouldn't take much to make a noise with those dry crispy leaves, just a couple of feet from my ears, and so if I want to drop off to sleep undisturbed it's safest to wear the ear plugs. Also the dawn chorus, currently at about 3.30am, pleasant noise though it is, is likely to wake me before I want to be woken.

I'm ready for an early night tonight, but first I've got to wash my pans, plates and cutlery in the bowl, and I've got to boil some water on the stove for that first. The light is fading as I put the washed pots and pans on the table to drain. The fire is dying too, just flickering a bit, with a few wisps of smoke drifting towards the sleeping tent. I decide to go to bed, getting undressed inside the tent and putting my boots in the porch. I'll leave out the ear plugs tonight so that I can hear the gentle sounds of Nature before I fall asleep. There's an owl hooting in the distance, then the flapping of wings up in the canopy as another bird settles down to roost. Also something rustling through the crispy dead holly leaves at the edge of the clearing. And as I lie there under the duvet in the dark there's just a faint orange flickering light coming from the fire, and the relaxing scent of wood smoke.

May Beauty Reign Over Utility

Flutter of wings – the robin comes to greet me. He flits between low branches and watches over me. It's another beautiful sunny morning, sunlight streaming through the trees, all manner of birdsong and a background hum of insects. Three small birds fly around together among the low branches, seemingly playing, maybe competing for food or sex. A grey squirrel scurries across the ground then along a low branch, pausing to look at me so that we briefly make eye contact. Those three birds again, flying around together – just playing I think. I will play on my own today. It would be good to have a playmate, but I can still enjoy myself without one.

Earlier I had my eyes closed as I was meditating – actually saying a little prayer, and when I opened them, for a brief moment I thought I saw a crowd of people watching me, but it was the trees. The trees were watching me, as I watched them. There was a reciprocity of perception. More than this, I strongly felt that we were of the same stuff, that we had a fellowship of being. I am becoming a part of the wood, and my experience of the wood is also the wood experiencing itself.

Now as I walk through the trees on the path to the track there are a number of slender dead beech branches leaning or bending away from the main trunk. I know that they would snap off easily at the base and could be sawn up for firewood, but I don't want to disturb this wild approach to the camp – partly because I want to leave as little evidence as possible that I am here, and partly because I like the 'jungle' appearance of it. There are two tall slim branches that lean towards each other at a forty-five degree angle, and where they meet near the top they have welded together. They are like close friends, inseparable now, and I wouldn't want to literally tear them apart for some utilitarian purpose that isn't even necessary. May beauty reign over utility.

I continue walking down the track to stretch my legs and get the long-range view. And just before the edge of the wood a large ash tree branch has broken from its trunk and fallen over the track. This must be the source of yesterday's 'crack, crack', and the branch must have come down in the night. The limb is not dead and looks healthy enough. Also the weather hasn't been wet or windy, so it's a bit of a mystery. The fact is that trees self-prune and it was just a matter of time. Why the tree chose to lose this particular limb I don't know, but I can only guess that it was compromising the symmetry of the whole. Just as we humans have to cast off the superfluous in our lives if we are to grow and to maintain a healthy integrity, the tree will have a blueprint life-plan, and this bough was no longer part of that plan.

The branch lies across the track, blocking the passage of vehicles. It's big and heavy and can't be moved by hand. Dorothy and her helpers won't be able to get out until it's been sawn up and removed. I can't help because I've got to go to work, and I've got to set off earlier than usual because I'm going to be in the Keswick shop today. Oh well, she's got Harry to see to it, and they could probably borrow the farmer's chainsaw. I text her to let her know and then continue walking down the track to get the view. And it's a mainly clear-blue sky, with a few patches of white cloud that are well above the summits. It's going to be a nice sunny day and I'll go for a run or walk somewhere after work in the shop.

The Other Side of the Raise

On the road now into Ambleside, instead of turning right at the top of Compston Road to park in my usual place by the Market Cross I turn left past The Climbers' Shop and Dodd's Restaurant to take the road to Keswick. This Ambleside to Keswick stretch of the A591 is probably my favourite road for driving in the whole of the Lakes. It's sixteen miles between the two towns, and it must be one of the most beautiful scenic drives in Britain. It's the main artery between South and North Lakes, the route going through Rydal and Grasmere, over Dunmail Raise, alongside Thirlmere and then over Nest Brow to Keswick.

Most people who live in the Lakes tend to stay in either the North or the South, and some view the other side with suspicion or dislike. 'Nowt good comes o'er t'Raise' is the old expression. Dunmail Raise was until 1974 the border between Cumberland in the north and Westmorland in the south. I think there is a slight difference in character between the people of the old counties, but it's been very much diluted these days by the influx of 'offcomers' on both sides. Still some people in South Lakes think that those in North Lakes are a bit backward or insular, and there are those in North Lakes who see South Lakes as being 'posh' or more commercialised than the North. I've lived on both sides of the Raise, I like them both and feel I belong to both. I started my Lakeland life in the North at Buttermere, and I feel a stronger attachment to the fells of North Lakes than to those of the South. Without doubt the fells are bigger and wilder in the North, and there's more of them to go at. But South Lakes has plenty of good fells too, and it's got its own charm. Certainly there are more trees, more woods in the South, which gives it a softer feel. I think perhaps it feels busier and more commercialised in the South because the roads get more clogged, especially the A591 between Windermere and Ambleside.

Anyway, I enjoy this drive up the A591, and it always feels like a little adventure going from one side to another, although I don't know on which side 'the grass is greener'. The fells are better in the North, but I know more people in the South. North of Grasmere I put the foot down to take the old Peugeot 306 as fast as it will go up the steady climb to Dunmail Raise, and then once over the top I can keep going at a fair pace. At this time in the morning there isn't too much traffic and I can enjoy the undisturbed view over Thirlmere now that the plantations have been felled. And so on, up to Swirls and down to The King's Head at Thirlspot, and then overtaking a couple of cars on the dual carriageway section. I go past Dale Bottom and then up the steep climb to Nest Brow, where at the top I get the fantastic view westwards to the Newlands Fells, north-west to Bassenthwaite Lake, and north to Skiddaw, with Keswick at its feet. It's a fantastic vista that's always exciting. And then it's the descent into town, past the lane to Castlerigg campsite on the left, then the right hand bend and into a thirty miles per hour zone as I drop into town, past the Penrith turn off, past the Twa Dogs Inn on the left and then into the town centre, past Station Road and Fitz Park on the right and then down the hill and round past the Post Office and the pedestrian crossing and then turning right up Stanger Street to find a parking space at the top.

And then I walk down the street into town to report for duty at the shop at 9am. And it's the same thing here as at the Ambleside shop, only this shop is bigger and is supposed to be a flagship store. It was refurbished over the winter and has only recently reopened, with all-new shop fittings and some more stock than at Ambleside. There's also a large screen behind the counter which shows a video taken from a plane or helicopter travelling across fields and then through some mountains in Scotland. I can't see the point of it myself, although I do know that people like to look at screens. The great outdoors on a screen is even better than the real thing for some people – you get the views without having to make any physical effort. The countryside is screened off, packaged and served up in a shop to the accompaniment of the same awful muzak we are subjected to in the Ambleside store. None of the staff here are remotely outdoorsy themselves, and one of them is off sick, which is why I'm here today to cover. You can understand why working here for long enough would make anyone sick, but 'it's a job' and people need jobs of some sort to pay the rent or please the parents or run the car or pay the bus fare from Workington to get to the job. Some people are better than others at putting up with crap jobs. Some are only too eager to turn themselves into compliant robots, especially if they are in a position to boss their colleagues about. The manager is a local girl who's resigned to her fate. A short fat lump of a thing with a sour face, she stands behind the counter going through the admin procedures on the till and comparing the store figures with those of Ambleside. She makes a bitchy comment about Sharon and ignores a customer who walks through the door. Then she asks me to put out some stock, to tidy the rails and serve customers. The usual stuff. I feel a bit more relaxed here than in the Ambleside store because it's not my usual place of work, I'm doing them a favour and I don't feel any pressure. However, I do feel a bit embarrassed to be here, especially when someone that I know comes into the store. I used to work with her at another outdoor shop in this town. It was a better one, although it was still a corporate chain with zero-hour contracts and an obsession with KPIs. It was better because the gear was mostly of good quality and the staff were genuinely outdoorsy. Anyway, when Lisa comes in and sees me I feel as if I've gone down in the world to this low-end shop, but I know that the staff at the old shop are not happy there, and it may be that she's having a look round here today because she's seen the staff vacancies sign in the shop window. Staff move from one shop to another, but as another colleague from the old shop put it: 'Same old shit, different shovel.'

At 1pm I can take my half hour lunch break. I head up Main Street into the Market Square, which is bustling with people, as usual. Keswick is much like Ambleside, only bigger, which is to say it's all about tourism, a 'honeypot' of outdoor shops, cafés, pubs, hotels and B&Bs. I walk past the Moot Hall, then turn left up Station Street and call in at the sandwich shop – where they have a huge range of fillings for your bread roll. I buy a hummus with salad and then walk further up the street, over the road and into the park, where I sit on a bench by the bowling green. By now I've only got fifteen minutes to eat my sandwich and get back to the shop. I watch a game of bowls in progress, which is pleasantly diverting and relaxing. And I think about my big running round, which I'm planning to do the day after tomorrow, which is a Friday. I had originally intended to do it on Sunday, but there's a weather front moving in and it's going to be very wet and windy with low cloud on the fells at the weekend, so I've brought it forward by a couple of days to take advantage of this fine sunny period whilst it lasts. I'd got a few lads to give me some running support on Sunday, but I wouldn't want to put us all through the bad weather because I want it to be an enjoyable day, rather than a grim ordeal with no views. Also I'd like to get round in a reasonable time. So I will now be running solo for the first two thirds, with roadside support from friends Ben and Christeen, and then I'll have Jim Tyson running with me on the third and final section. I've got a crate of stuff in my car that I'll take round to Ben's house in Keswick after work – some spare clothes, food and drink, and he'll have this crate in his car when he and Christeen meet me at a few points on the round.

Anyway, it's back to work in the shop and so I get up from the bench and walk back through town. The afternoon passes tolerably as I put out some stock in the camping section upstairs. Most of the product is of very poor quality and over-priced for what it is, and I don't like selling such stuff because in so doing I am implicated in the dishonesty of the company, but of course that's what I'm paid to do. 'How waterproof are these boots?' a customer may ask, to which the correct answer to achieve a sale would be 'fully waterproof', but to which a more honest answer would be 'hardly waterproof at all.' I am honest with customers, even though it doesn't help sales figures, and it reveals my basic lack of trust in a company that thrives on misleading gullible people in its pricing strategies and in its product descriptions. Such business practices are common, if not almost standard, on the high street, and some retail workers might say 'that's just how it is' and get on with it uncomplainingly. But I find the whole culture of dishonesty, poor quality, and sales and profit above all else sickens me. I'd rather work for an independent outdoor shop that sells quality gear and cares more about its customers and its staff, and I've worked at such shops in the past, but for the time being this is all I could get. This place is hardly even a real outdoor shop, but more a leisure wear or 'lifestyle' clothing shop. Here you are expected to perform like a monkey to achieve the KPI targets of the company. You have to be seen to be keeping busy, putting on an act and wearing a mask – a happy smiling face to generate sales. 'Have a nice day, guys!'

And so I exchange several hours of my time for a paltry wage that I've got to wait for weeks on end to receive. It's a lovely summer's day, the shop is quiet and I'm told I can go at 4pm. And I'm glad to get outside, back into the sun. I'm going to go for a walk up Newlands, but first I'll take the crate around to Ben's. He's texted me to say he'll be out walking today, so I won't see him and I'll leave it in his back yard shed.

The Purple House

After dropping off the crate I drive out of town to the A66, then turn off at Portinscale and take the road up the Newlands Valley – past Lingholm, then the Swinside Inn, Stair and finally to Rigg Beck, where I park around the back of the big stone house, rather than in the old quarry. There's a little patch of common land here, just down from the ford and the footbridge over the beck. It's pretty overgrown with weeds here nowadays, but there's just space for a car or two. It's an interesting spot historically. There was an ancient corn mill here, then later the Mill Dam farm/public house (aka The Dog and Gun, then later The Sportsman Inn), which was used by the local farmers, as well as some visitors. But when the wooden clapboard-style Newlands Hotel was built in 1888 the Sportsman Inn closed. Even back then the tourist trade was starting to dominate Lakeland life, and The Newlands Hotel was a stopping off point for the increasing number of visitors on the coach and horse 'circular' from Keswick to Buttermere via Honister and Newlands Pass. The hotel was also the venue for many vale celebrations, anniversary meals and post-funeral teas, but by the 1950s it stood empty for a few years – until it was purchased by the Vergauwens as a family home and became the purple-painted 'Rigg Beck', named after the stream that runs by the house. Later, as the family broke up, it became a lodging house run by the eccentric 'Mrs. Vee'. The house attracted a number of writers and also actors working at the old Blue Box Theatre in Keswick. Guests included Alan Sillitoe, Shelagh Delaney, Victoria Wood and Bob Hoskins, but the most famous of all was Ted Hughes, who came to stay at the house for a few weeks after Sylvia Plath died. I lived at the house myself in the summer of '93, then again in '96, and the spring of 2000. I came to write and it was a good place to do that, being in a quiet, idyllic spot, away from the madding crowds of Keswick, and right in the fells – nestling at the foot of Causey Pike. When I wasn't writing or working at some job or another in town or at the Swinside Inn I would go running or walking in the surrounding fells.

In the summer of '96 I bought my Lichfield Viper ridge tent from a camping exhibition in town and vaguely thought about camping up the Rigg Beck valley but never got around to it. With a room at the Purple House I didn't feel the need. I was well set up in the Red Room, which was living pretty close to Nature as it was. However, the tent came in useful in subsequent years – on my days off when I was warden at Black Sail Hut in Ennerdale, then later when I used to visit the hut when Pete was the warden and I would camp in the drumlins and get my dinner at the hostel. Later still I used it when I was camping at the site in Grizedale, then at Rascal How in the Coniston Fells.

Mrs Vee finally had to move out in the noughties due to ill health. At this stage the house was in a very poor state of repair and was shored up with scaffolding. A property developer bought the house in 2007 and it was subsequently, mysteriously and conveniently burnt down the following year, making way for a new house to be built in its place. The new house, also called 'Rigg Beck', is built of stone and looks like a ship, being a long oblong, curved at both ends and with two big chimney pots like funnels and a few porthole-style windows. The window into the open plan kitchen/dining area is huge, but the blind is nearly always down as the place seems to be only lived in for a few weeks of the year. It's a holiday home – perhaps for the wealthy man who bought the old wooden purple house, reportedly a stockbroker from Kingston-upon-Thames. Architecturally the building is impressive, but I don't think it fits in as well as the old purple house did, and it doesn't look very homely. It may be constructed of traditional stone, but it looks to me more like a restaurant or an art gallery, and something that would look less out of place in town. The front door has been painted purple – as a nod to the old house, and the words 'RIGG BECK' are in stainless steel letters in a modern bold but soulless font attached to the pale wooden slats at one side. Above the door is a CCTV camera. All in all the place lacks character, soul. The purple front door is the only good thing about it, and it's a far cry from the old purple house, which may have been ramshackle, but the door was always open and it provided accommodation for local people of limited means, many of them creative in one way or another. Now we have this new stone house, imposing itself on the landscape, the ostentatious architectural 'grand design' of someone with no connection to the area and which is only lived in for a few weeks of the year. It's a snub to people like me, and it's typical of the way things have gone in the Lakes – more and more places being bought up as second homes and nowhere affordable to live for the workers – which is why I am having to live in a tent. The Lake District has become a less interesting place as a result of younger, materially poorer people being squeezed out by older wealthier people, most of them from outside the area. The old purple house didn't just attract young people, but *creative* people, *alternative* people, but such people hardly seem to exist anymore around here – where the culture is simply one of getting and spending and playing in the outdoors. The Lake District has become increasingly monied-class and increasingly shallow.

Anyway, this spot is where I used to park last summer, when I was camping up the Rigg Beck valley. After a day in the shop I would drive up here, maybe go for a run and wash myself in the beck, then set up my table and chair and make some sort of meal, drink a couple of bottles of beer and sit and enjoy the view over the valley to Cat Bells. Then I'd wash my pots in the beck, put everything back in the boot of the car and walk up the lane past the house, over the road bridge at the hairpin bend, then take the narrow path beside the beck, through the gorse bushes and the high bracken, following this path up the valley for about twenty minutes until I reached a broken down sheepfold and a flat grassy area beside the beck. My tent was pitched there, and it's where I slept for three weeks, before decamping in the middle of the night during a wild storm when the gusting gale force wind was threatening to blow the tent away and take me with it.

Today I'll walk up the valley to where I camped, then maybe go up to Ard Crags or just walk back down the valley. As I walk past the new house I remember that when it was being built I had a snoop round and found the old iron fingerpost road sign in the outhouse. It was the sign that must have once stood at the top of the lane, indicating 'Little Town', 'Buttermere' and 'Keswick', but which some purple house wit had painted over with 'HERE', 'THERE' and 'EVERYWHERE' on one side and 'YOUR WAY', 'MY WAY' and 'THE WAY' on the other side. I thought about taking it away as a souvenir of the spirit of the old house, but it was too big and heavy to put in my car, besides which I didn't have anywhere to put it where I was renting a room. It probably ended up at a scrap metal merchants in Workington and was melted down – evidence of the good old days destroyed.

The old Purple House represented wildness and freedom – an alternative to the tame sheepfold of town, where all rooms must be centrally-heated and en-suite, all lawns must be dandelion-free, and conversations revolve around property prices and foreign holidays. A bit of distance from civilisation can give a sense of freedom and a healthy, creative perspective. A more enlightened perspective perhaps.

Being closer to Nature has a lot to do with it, and the wilder the Nature the better.

I turn right at the top of the lane and walk down the hill to the hairpin bend and the bridge, then turn left up the track beside the beck, just before the old quarry. At first it's like a tunnel through gorse bushes and bracken, but then it opens up and contours up the valley beside the beck down on the left. I first started walking and running up here when I lived at the Purple House, and there's something about this path that holds a strong appeal for me, perhaps just from having so much personal history of going up here many times over the years, or perhaps also because there is something about this bit of fellscape that speaks to my soul in a way that is impossible to define but which is in some way meaningful. I remember that years ago the words 'disappear into the landscape' came to mind whilst running up here, and there is that feeling of going into the wild, of being embosomed by the fells, of losing oneself in the landscape, of self and environment becoming one.

Disappear into the Landscape

Walking along the path my eyes are drawn up to the steep cone of Causey Pike ahead, and to the ridge of Ard Crags rising steeply to the left. These fells rise up from the valley with a fairy-tale beauty, a gracefulness of form which somehow makes me feel 'at home'. The path climbs gently and curves round a contour of the fell, which rises steeply on my right. There are a few places where the path has become waterlogged and I have to take a small detour above it. It didn't used to be like this until a few years ago, and it's interesting how quickly things can change in the fell environment. Up on the high tops things change very little but down in the valleys there are subtle changes happening all the time.

After ten minutes walking the path curves round and the view becomes a bit more desolate. Ard Crags rises steeply on the left, Causey Pike on the right, and up ahead the path climbs steeply and invitingly up through scree slopes, with the hump of Sail now framed in the v-gap at the head of the valley. Above the path, high on the slopes of Causey and Scar Crags, is a patch of woodland, mainly stunted sessile oaks, a remnant of the ancient forest that once covered the whole of the Lake District, such that only the high peaks peeped above it. Centuries of tree-felling and sheep-grazing have reduced the Lakeland fellscape to being something of a desert of mainly grass, bracken, heather and bare rock, so it's good to see these trees hanging on in there at what must be the upper limit for them: a reminder of what was once the natural environment of the Lake District thousands of years ago.

A little further on and I can see the spot where I camped beside the beck. It's not as good a place as it was because the flat grassy area is strewn with rocks that have been washed down during a storm, and the old sheepfold has broken down some more. I find a tent peg beside a rock – one that I must've left behind when I quickly evacuated the site in the middle of the night. In a way it seems a strange choice for a longish-term wild camp with it being so close to, and visible from, the public footpath. But this path, which runs over the hause to Buttermere, is not overly popular. From what I've seen you tend to get either older walkers or D of E groups taking this route, which stays below the fell tops, but which provides a good direct route between Buttermere and Newlands. The site is not visible from any farms or houses and is not accessible by motor vehicle because the path is far too narrow. Nevertheless, I did feel a bit exposed, and every time I walked up here there was a slight fear and real possibility that the tent might not be there anymore – that somebody might have stolen it. I actually put a note in the porch area: I AM NOT ON

HOLIDAY. I WORK IN KESWICK AND THIS TENT IS MY ONLY HOME – an explanation to any self-appointed 'fell-police' and a plea to any potential thieves. Another disadvantage of this spot was that the sun would drop down behind Sail relatively early in the evening, and it would get quite chilly. But at 7am in the morning the sun would appear from behind Rowling End and shine onto the tent, just as I was getting up – so that was nice. I had a fire on a couple of evenings, using logs that I'd sawn myself from a dead tree up on the steep lower slopes of Ard Crags, and I would sit on my tripod stool, warming my hands, maybe drinking a can of beer and looking down the valley towards the ridge of Cat Bells, which was still in the sun. And sometimes I would make a simple meal up here, rather than down at the car – maybe tinned soup and bread, and I would sit in splendid isolation – to the gentle musical accompaniment of running water in the beck. The place was a bit bleak – not exactly a sublime mountain arena, but secluded enough, and peaceful. It was only twenty minutes from the road, but it felt like in the middle of nowhere. Before I camped here I tried some other wild camping spots up the valley of Newlands Beck, between High Spy and Hindscarth, but they were too much of a walk in from the car to combine with going out to work at the shop, and so I chose this place for its accessibility as much as anything.

Right now I wonder where to go from here. One way or another I want to keep walking and enjoying this late-afternoon sun. I could carry on up this valley to the hause, then strike up the side of Ard Crags and then descend down the steep ridge back this way – but I've done that so many times before. I look up to the patch of woodland on the steep slope below Scar Crags and decide to have a bit of a challenge and explore up there. I get back onto the path and walk a little further up the valley before heading straight up the very steep fellside and aiming for a shoot of scree. It's hard work through deep heather, and it doesn't get any easier when I reach the shifting stones of the scree, but this at least provides a clear way through the heather. At the top of the scree there are two sheep, a ewe and a lamb, resting, sunbathing and smiling in the sun, and I wonder why they've chosen to come all the way up here – perhaps in search of succulent green treats in the wood. And now I enter the wood – a tangle of stunted gnarly old trees, mainly oaks, clinging to the steep fellside. I stop for a rest, sit on a mossy boulder and attune to my surroundings. It's like an untouched world up here, a place where no-one goes, but a little haven for wildlife. My ears are filled with birdsong, and I see a small mammal, a stoat perhaps, dart between the boulders and heather. This is a bit of land that time forgot, a little example of how the fells used to look thousands of years ago, a remnant from another age, a patch of true wildwood. It's way off the usual walking routes and very few people would consider going up here because it's very hard to get to, and where would you go from here?

I decide to carry on upwards to the top of the ridge at Scar Crags, but this gets ever steeper and more difficult – a scramble up through rocks and heather, grasping at the woody heather stalks to haul myself up, feeling for firm ground beneath my feet, the stones shifting with each step. I'm sweating profusely in this late afternoon heat, and progress is slow and challenging, to say the least. I try to find the easiest line, but it's all difficult. At one point I get out of the heather and scramble up the bare rock of a small crag. It's nice to feel the warm dry rock in my hands, and also the little frisson of exposure, but I have to be careful because I'm not really a climber. My heart pounds with the danger, as well as the exertion. This is probably the craziest route I've ever taken up a Lake District fell, and I'm starting to question the wisdom of doing this. There is a feeling of no-one ever having been this way before. Who in their right mind would choose such a route? It's perhaps a bit like fell-walking five thousand years ago, but even then no-one would choose to come up here. It's nothing but hard work, difficulty, awkwardness – but there is that reward of being somewhere that is truly wild, untouched by human presence and untouched even by sheep.

Finally, and with a great sense of relief, I attain the crest of the ridge and look down into the valley to the beck glinting in the sun. I turn right and stroll along the ridge to Causey Pike, from where I take the path down over Rowling End, dropping down to the road, and then it's just a short walk back to the car. I'm feeling quite satisfied with my challenging foray into the wild, and also thirsty for a beer or two – so I drive back through Stair and up to the Swinside Inn.

The Swinside Inn

Now sitting in the beer garden at the Swinny I have the place almost to myself, except for a self-contained family group on the other side. I'm happy that it's quiet, but then again I am sociable and it would be good to chat with some fellow souls, folk appreciating the place, the fells, and folk who might have something interesting to say. I saw a sign outside the new Wetherspoons in town that said 'Reject isolation, join the congregation... at the pub', which made me smile. Most people in there were staring at their smart phones, locked into their virtual social worlds. Some people enjoy a solitary reflective pint and some people enjoy isolation – to a degree, but we are all sociable creatures at the end of the day and too much isolation is not a good thing. A life without friends is no life at all and the fells, much as I love them, are not really friends.

Beer is not a friend either, although sometimes it seems to be so, and a life without beer would not be much of a life for me. A pint of Jennings Cumberland Ale sits on the wooden table before me, a deep golden ale topped with a quarter inch of creamy head. I pick up the glass and hold it aloft to the western sun so that the sunlight shines through it, illuminating a clarity of content. And then I raise the glass to my mouth and gulp down a goodly amount of the stuff, tasting a good balance of hoppy and malty flavours and refreshing a thirst brought on by a day of working in the shop, followed by my wild walk.

That pint goes down very quickly and I take the empty glass with me back to the bar for another one. This pub has long been on my radar – ever since I first lived at the Purple House a mile or so up the valley back in '93. That was twenty-one years ago and I still keep being drawn back to the Swinside. It hasn't changed very much since then, although different managers have come and gone. Inside it's a traditional olde worlde Lakeland pub with low beams, photographs and paintings of local scenes, a fireplace and an ancient-looking dark wooden piece of furniture, a sideboard, which one of the staff told me is over four hundred years old. Outside is a beer garden with spacious views across the Newlands Valley to the fells, and if you sit in the right place you can see pretty much the whole of the Newlands skyline – with Cat Bells, Maiden Moor, Hindscarth, Robinson, Causey Pike and Barrow. It's not so much a garden as an outside seating area next to the car parking area but it's a good place to sit and contemplate over a late-afternoon or early evening pint or two, especially when the sun is shining. It can get busy but usually it feels like a world away from the crowds of Keswick.

I actually worked here about fourteen years ago, whilst living at the Purple House and trying to work on my book *Black Sail*. It was the last days of the Purple House, things were very difficult there with Mrs. Vee and I had to move out after only a couple of months. I had to leave my kitchen assistant job at the Swinny too, but it was no great loss as I hadn't enjoyed working under the bad-tempered chef who was there at the time.

Anyway, it's time to head back to South Lakes, back home to the wood – though I'll stop in Ambleside to go to the chippy.

There's a queue at the Walnut Fish Bar but the Polish staff behind the counter are very efficient and I don't have to wait long for my cheese and onion pie with chips and mushy peas – which I take away in the paper carrier bag to eat on a bench by the church. I walk down the lane past the primary school into the churchyard, then around the back of the church to a wooden bench facing the park and Loughrigg Fell, although the view is obscured by bushes. It's a nice quiet spot where I can eat in peace, with an inquisitive blackbird for company. The sun's gone down now and it's getting quite chilly, but this hot food will warm me up.

One lunchtime I sat in this spot with a sandwich when a hearse came driving slowly past, the first vehicle in a little funeral convoy. It was quite a shock as I didn't realise that cars could drive all the way around the church – but there we are, a little reminder of mortality as I sat there feeding myself, still in good health and good spirits, but aware that these things will not last forever.

Pleasantly full from my pie, chips and peas I drive back to the wood, via a shower at the National Trust campsite en route, and when I finally get back it's almost dark. I decide not to bother with a fire, so just make a mug of herbal tea and retire to the tent, where I sit cross-legged at the high end and read a little of Roger Deakin's *Notes from Walnut Tree Farm* by the light of a small lantern suspended from a loop on the polyester 'ceiling', before undressing, getting under the duvet and turning out the light.

True Wealth, Freedom and Beauty

Another warm dry morning, although the sun is shrouded by high white cloud. I slept well after my day at the Keswick shop, followed by the walk from Rigg Beck, and I was in no hurry to get out of bed so lay there 'til about 7.30am, feeling well rested and peaceful. Now sitting under the tarp, having had my breakfast, I'm having my morning contemplation – just sitting quietly, staring into the trees. I listen to the birdsong, and also to the rapid-fire drumming of a woodpecker. The woodpecker noise is quite close and I get up from my chair to see if I can spot the bird. I scan the nearby trees and catch a glimpse of some white plumage up high. And there it is – a great spotted woodpecker climbing a dead trunk, pausing to tap here and there, then jack-hammering at the bark. For such an energetic and violent beak-action the sound produced is strangely peaceful – more like a creaking than a hammering. It's a sound I often hear in the wood and it's somehow reassuring.

Today is more or less a day off from the shop as I'm just going in for a couple of hours of lunchtime cover. I want to go to the launderette and the library in

Ambleside and also have a bit of a walk, but not too much as I need to have an easy day before my big round tomorrow.

The launderette is on the premises of what was once Johnny Williamson's barber shop, and the proprietor has left the old 'Barber' wording above the window, which must be confusing to some visitors. There's a sign on the door saying 'OPPEN', which is a Cumbrian pronunciation of open, and when the place is not oppen it's 'CLOTHESD'. The lady who runs this place has a sense of humour. Anyway, I load up a machine, insert my coins and set the thing going. The cycle lasts about half an hour, so I'll go to the library whilst I'm waiting.

At the library I am greeted by Chris, who seems to be the main man here these days. I first met him a couple of years ago when he came to visit Dorothy at the house and he was thinking of living there as her helper – to replace me, but he thought better of it. He'd had a live-in kitchen position at an outdoor centre but was made redundant, but then he got this job at the library, which suits him just fine. He's a single chap, about the same age as me, and he too has struggled to find accommodation in the area and is staying temporarily in a friend's caravan in Grasmere.

I get myself a computer in the back room and log on to check my email, Facebook, and to look for accommodation and jobs online. I also check the all-important weather forecast, which is still looking good for tomorrow. And I look at the website gofar.org.uk, which lists various ultra-distance challenges in the upland areas of the UK, and to which my 'Freeman Round' might be added, once I've done it. The site provides some good inspiration for running big rounds and is well put together by Tony and Richard Wimbush. On one page there's a 'Health Warning', and I think this captures the spirit behind undertaking these endeavours quite nicely:

To do any of these routes on this site is not normal, sensible or rational. They will appeal most to those whose horizons stretch way beyond the urban wastelands of our celebrity culture and our mindless consumerism, past the swamps of our political malaise and way beyond the arid deserts of religious or scientific fundamentalism. For a while at least, these routes will allow you to experience true wealth, freedom and beauty by stepping outside the narrow confines of normal thinking and living in a semi-wilderness where everything is free to anyone with a little time, effort and awareness!

Back at the launderette the wash cycle has finished and I transfer my clothes into a tumble drier, insert some coins and push the start button. I've got some time to kill and I can't just sit here and watch my clothes tumble round so I get a takeaway coffee from the bakery on the other side of the road, and an 'i' newspaper from Stobbart's newsagent at the bottom of the road, on the corner. The traffic coming into Ambleside is building up now, with a tailback of slow-moving cars stretching down past White Platts Recreation Ground to the mini-roundabout. I take my paper and coffee back to the launderette and read about the latest in the world of politics and current affairs. It's mostly depressing reading and sometimes I wonder why I bother reading newspapers, but I do like to keep myself informed to some extent about what's going on in the world. I read a story about some war or atrocity in a faraway country, or about the state of the UK economy, and sometimes I have an emotional response or I form an opinion, but it's nearly all irrelevant to my day-to-day life, the people that I meet and the things that I do. And rather than worry about things over which I have no control it's better to focus on 'my own backyard'. And I think of that prayer: 'God grant me the serenity to accept the things I cannot change, courage to change the things I can, and wisdom to know the difference.'

I've drunk my coffee, read some of the newspaper and now my clothes are dry, so I pile them up in a large carrier bag and take them to the car. I've got some more time before I go to work at the shop, so I go to Granny Smiths wholefood shop to stock up on some small cartons of soya milk, brown rice and dried fruit bars, then I go to the Picnic Box, where I get my usual cheese ploughman's roll for lunch. And then I call at the children's outdoor shop to say hello to Julie, who's sat at the desk, staring at the computer, perhaps planning her next cycle touring adventure or updating her blog or tweeting someone on Twitter. Like me she doesn't like working in outdoor retail, but she's got quite a cushy number here, working on her own usually and often doing her own thing on the internet in between customers. She lives in the middle of Ambleside but finds the crowds get to her and she longs to get away into the wilds on her bike and with her tent. Strangely she doesn't explore the Lakes much, preferring to go up to Scotland or Scandinavia for a big annual trip. She set up a blog and has got quite a following for her adventures, which are supposed to be empowering for other women who venture into the great outdoors. She's also a runner and a wild swimmer and we've had a couple of swims together in Rydal Water.

But now it's time for me to go to my 'own' shop for a couple of hours work. Two hours of serving customers and tidying up clothes on rails passes tolerably and is a few more quid earned before I go back into the sunshine. I sit on a bench in the courtyard to eat my sandwich and listen to the busker girl who's singing and strumming a guitar outside the Lakeland clothing shop. And very pleasant it is too. I've not seen a busker here before but it's good and I think Ambleside needs more of this – a bit of real live music performance rather than the piped muzak in the shops. It's a bit of creativity and culture, a good healthy diversion from the getting and spending of the 'retail experience'. She sings beautifully and she plays the guitar well, and when I've finished my sandwich and she's finished a song I go up and drop a pound coin into her hat on the ground.

The time is now 2.30pm and I set off for a bit of a walk. I head up North Road and then turn up Nook Lane, which takes me up behind the old Charlotte Mason College, now University of Cumbria campus. Further up I pass the Greenbank housing estate, a couple of B&Bs, the foxhound kennels up on the right, and then Nook End farm. I go through a couple of gates then take the bridge over Scandale Beck and drop down a meadow, through a small wood to the Rydal Hall track. And I follow this track to Rydal Hall, where I pass through the campsite.

Outside the toilet block there's a young man ironing his tee-shirts on a picnic mat, his iron plugged into an extension lead leading to a socket inside the building. I say to him 'I've seen it all now', but he doesn't seem at all embarrassed, as if ironing one's clothes at a campsite was quite normal. But surely camping and ironing are two things that don't really go together. The iron is a symbol of domestication, and camping is supposed to be about getting away from that. But in these days of 'glamping' people like to bring all the comforts of home with them – 'everything but the kitchen sink', including their electric iron so that they can look smart doing whatever it is they are here to do – bimbling about Ambleside, fiddling with their smartphone, going out for dinner or whatever.

Why do people iron clothes? Traditionally for work in a job, a 'white collar' job, or for a job interview or for Sunday church service or special occasions such as weddings or funerals. But these days people might iron pretty much all their clothes, their jeans, tee-shirts – their everyday wear. It's perhaps a form of neuroticism, the desire for neat straight lines and no creases. The ironed shirt is like the manicured suburban lawn – managed, controlled. Just as there is a fear of things going wild in the garden, there is a fear of creases in one's garments.

I continue my walk past Rydal Hall, down the lane to the busy A591, where I turn left, follow the road for a bit, then turn right over Pelter Bridge to take the Under Loughrigg road. There are lots of walkers along here and it's a pleasant route back to Ambleside, though you have to watch out for cyclists and cars. The road passes some big and beautiful houses as it meanders around the foot of Loughrigg Fell. At one point there's a footpath on the right that leads steeply up onto the fell, and some ten years ago I camped up there for a few weeks to escape from the noise of the shared house in Millans Park where I was renting a room. I found the late-evening comings and goings and cooking in the kitchen next to my room very irritating and stressful, so I would retreat to my tent halfway up the fell beside a stream for a restful night's sleep. I suppose I'm not well-suited to living in shared houses, especially when I'm sharing with young noisy people who keep late hours. I've had so many unhappy experiences in shared houses and I'd rather live in my tent in the wood than pay a lot of rent for another unhappy house-share.

Further along the road I pass the steep lane that heads up Loughrigg, and where I'll be heading early tomorrow morning for the first leg of my round. Then it's over the cattle grid and the little hump-backed stone bridge into Rothay Park and back into the village, up Compston Road, then up the ginnel past the Rattle Gill café to North Road, and then into the beer garden of The Golden Rule pub. It's a nice sun-trap here in the mid-afternoon and I want to just sit for a while in the sun with a pint or two. I go in the back door and get a pint of Dizzy Blonde from barman Steve, then take it back outside to the wooden table and just sit there sunning myself and drinking slowly. Landlord John comes out to collect some empty glasses and asks me how I am. I tell him that I'm doing my big round tomorrow, which actually starts and finishes here at the Rule, so I'll maybe see him tomorrow evening when I get back. 'Very good' he says, and takes a load of empty glasses inside.

And then I get into conversation with a couple at the next table who have walked round the Fairfield Horseshoe today. This pub is good for going on your own and just striking up conversation with people about walking or whatever. There's a good friendly convivial atmosphere where people are happy to talk to strangers about where they are from, where they've been walking and where they are staying etc. I spend a pleasant hour drinking two pints of Dizzy and chatting to people, before heading back to my car and then driving back to the wood, where I'll have a relatively early meal and then go to bed early in preparation for my early start tomorrow.

Back at camp I put some wholegrain rice on to boil and chop some veggies, whilst listening to the birds and also to Radio 6. I make a simple spicy veg stew to go with the rice, which I eat sitting under the tarp and staring into the trees. And I think about tomorrow – my big day on the fells, which I first conceived years ago, and which I've been planning in detail and training for over the last few months. I've never run such a distance before so it's a bit of a step into the unknown, but I should be all right. The furthest I've run on my recces is the section from Ambleside to Keswick, which is 27 miles and 8,000 feet of climbing. There is a slight fear that I may 'blow up' or get cramp and be unable to complete it. Then again I am well-prepared with food and support and the many miles of training I've done. I wash up my pans and plate, make a herbal tea, read a little Roger Deakin then retire to the tent, get under the duvet and, even though it's still not quite dark, I soon drop off to sleep.

A Sense of Belonging

Driving along the road to Ambleside at 5.45am and listening to the album *Funhouse* by The Stooges, I've got the volume cranked up and I'm psyching myself up for today's fifty mile run around the Lakeland fells. I find the music really exciting, especially the first three tracks, and this has to be one of the best rock albums ever made – released back in 1970 but hugely influential on punk, which came several years later. It has the spirit of punk, a really strong energy – raw, visceral, feral, vital. Iggy Pop whoops and yowls and growls menacingly, the drumming is brutal and relentless, the guitars are scorching and the singing is passionate and wild. This music has the power to put me in a good mental state for fell-running. By some alchemy it gives me energy, altering my mental state like some kind of shamanic ritual, transmitting its madness into me – a particular kind of mad energy that corresponds to the madness required to run up and down mountains. To be honest it's the kind of listening that is probably best suited to fell-*racing*, rather than the ultra-distance challenge, but nevertheless I think it's a good way to start this special fell-running day.

The road is quiet and I arrive in Ambleside at 6am. I turn up the Kirkstone road and drive past The Golden Rule, then turn off right to park just below the old St. Anne's Church. I had intended to set off on the run at 6am, but getting prepared before I set off in the car took a little longer than expected. I got up at about 4.45am, had my usual breakfast of banana, muesli and black coffee and organised my kit for the day. Now I just need to strip down to my tee-shirt and shorts, put my fell shoes on and strap on my rucksack and bum bag. I also spend a bit of time checking the contents of the rucksack – which contains water-proofs, hat and gloves, food and water etc. The bum bag contains a waterproof bag which has my neatly-written schedule and a short pencil for noting my actual times at each summit or other 'checkpoint'. I lock up the car, check my trusty Casio digital watch – 6.15am, note the start time on my schedule, slide the schedule back into the waterproof bag, zip up the bum bag and spin it round to my back. And then I set off at a gentle trot down the road.

It's a beautiful morning with the sun breaking through the patches of mist on the fells. At the mini-roundabout I turn right and jog along Rydal Road, past the car park and police station, then turn left down Stoney Lane. The end of the lane becomes a pleasant tree lined path with a sports field on the right. A young man wearing a bowler hat and carrying a fishing rod is walking across the field. He sees me running and shouts over 'Are you going up there?' – pointing in the direction of Loughrigg. 'Yes,' I say. 'And some more...' 'I've just been up there and I couldn't see my hand in front of my face,' he says. He looks odd with his bowler hat – different to the people you usually see around here, not that you usually see many folk around at this time in the morning. I thought I was making an early start, but the man in the bowler hat beat me to it.

I'm feeling okay in myself, although I'm not used to running this early in the day. I can feel my breakfast in my belly, but I'm only going at a slow trot along this path, then over the footbridge, turn right, over the cattle grid and then turn left up the steep lane that leads towards Loughrigg. I slow to a walk up this steep slope. There's no rush and I've got to conserve my energy. On my schedule I've allowed 35 minutes to get from The Golden Rule to the top of Loughrigg, and that includes some walking. It's a bit different to when I took part in the Loughrigg race a couple of months ago. Then it was a mad charge out of Rothay Park, the hump-backed footbridge a bottleneck for eager competitors trying to get past one another, and then this steep tarmac climb with space to overtake, some over-eager starters already breathless and slowing right down, others gradually forging ahead, steadily overtaking, and some hanging on to their position, keeping in contention with some marker competitor of about their own standard. Racing is fun: the thrill of the chase gets the adrenaline going and you push yourself as hard as you can – and hopefully have a bit of 'crack' along the way, or at least afterwards. But sometimes it seems to be just an ego-driven herd stampede, where the object of the exercise is simply to go as fast as you can and beat as many other competitors as you can. It's a very different experience to the solitary fell run that is undertaken primarily as a communion with the fell environment or as a challenge that is measured purely by one's own standards. Although I've enjoyed racing (and hope to continue to do so) and also going for social fell runs, the most important fell-running experience for me is the solitary run, and especially the *long* run.

Over twenty-three years ago I moved to Ambleside and rented a room in a house in Millans Park owned by legendary fell-runner Keith Anderson. Prior to this I'd been working for the Youth Hostels Association in the Lakes for a few years and had done quite a bit of fell-running, mostly on my own, although I had done a handful of races. When I moved to Ambleside I joined the running club, Ambleside AC, and I became serious about training and racing. Keith was the team captain and used to lead us on tough training sessions in preparation for the races of the British Championship, which became the main racing focus for the club. On dark winter evenings we used to do punishing hill rep sessions on the streets around Ambleside, or else straight hard ten mile runs on the country lanes. After Tuesday evening runs we would often go for a couple of pints at The Golden Rule. Once the racing season got underway in the spring the training was on the fell and geared to whatever races were coming up. On Tuesday evenings and Sunday mornings we would meet at various pubs in South Lakes, go for our two-hour run and then go for a drink. And we would travel to races as a club, some local, some in the Peak

District, Wales, Scotland and elsewhere. Keith was an enthusiastic captain and he quickly became the star of the club and led us to British Championship victory that year. The great thing about Keith was that just a few years previously he'd been an overweight cigarette-smoking chef – until he discovered the sport of fell-racing, which pretty much transformed his life. He trained and raced 'like a demon' – especially when descending. He lost a lot of weight and made himself ill through over-training and under-eating, but then bounced back even stronger and faster. He continued to work as a chef at a restaurant in Ambleside, but was lucky enough to negotiate a Monday-to-Friday working week to fit round his fell-racing.

That first year I lived in Ambleside wasn't just about the fell-running for me. The village was a vibrant place to be, with jobs in the shops, cafés and pubs filled by mainly young people from all over this country who'd moved to the area to pursue their outdoor activities on the fells, crags and biking trails. There were more students here then too (before the local Charlotte Mason College got swallowed up by the University of Cumbria). I worked initially as a cook at Zeffirellis and saw myself as setting out on a career as a vegetarian chef – but that didn't last long as the owner got rid of me after only a few weeks, ostensibly because of 'staffing costs', but perhaps because he didn't like my style of cooking. There then followed a string of jobs: outdoor shop, council gardener, waiter, kitchen porter, off-licence, health food shop, the Spar shop etc. For a while I combined two or three jobs to make ends meet. There were jobs galore, all poorly-paid of course, but there was always some kind of work going and I met a lot of interesting people along the way. That first year I spent in Ambleside made a big impression on me and gave me a sense of belonging to the place, such that it always feels like home when I come back here. I have a fondness for it, even in the height of summer when the streets are thronged with tourists.

As well as changing jobs a lot I changed addresses a few times and found it hard to find a good place where I could settle. My desire to write was growing and I bought a second-hand typewriter, but I struggled to find a quiet room to do it, besides which I was still struggling to formulate what it was I wanted to say. My latter days in the village – or 'town', as some would have it – were spent in a dingy but cheap room at Bill Peel's Loughrigg View house, just down from The Golden Rule. I was working part-time at the Spar shop and didn't have enough money to live, so I decided to return to the YHA and got a job for the season at Ingleton in the Yorkshire Dales. Thus began another life-chapter, but I remained in close contact with the Lakes, continuing to race for Ambleside AC and returning to live in the village a few years later.

On a Spiritual Path

Running now on the rough stony track past the house called 'Pine Rigg' (which was once the clubhouse of a golf course, although it's hard to imagine that there was once a golf course here) and on up the track, through a swing gate, then veering off right onto the grass and picking up a soggy path that curves and then climbs up through the new season's bracken and heads in a fairly direct line for Loughrigg. It's surprising at this time of year how quickly the bracken grows. Just a few weeks ago there was none, but now it's getting fairly high. It has a distinctive smell – sharp, slightly bitter but not unpleasant. It's the familiar smell of the fells in summer. The fresh green fronds brush against my bare legs, which is a nice sensation, except that I worry these days about picking up ticks and so I avoid it wherever possible and check myself for the tiny black creatures when I stop for a moment. There is the worry of Lyme disease, to which a couple of fell-runners I know have succumbed in recent years.

Onwards and upwards, and I feel like I'm starting to get into the run now I've warmed up a bit. There's the final steep climb to the summit, then when I reach the trig point I spin my bum bag around and take out my schedule to note my time of arrival: 6.51. That means it's taken me one minute more than the thirty-five minutes I scheduled for this leg. That's close enough and I'm more or less on schedule and it's a good start. There's a good view from here of the fells all around. The sun is filtered slightly through some wispy high white cloud, but strong enough to have burned off most of the patches of mist on the tops and in the valleys. There's hardly any wind; everything is calm and it feels like a benevolent sort of day. I can't see another human being, although I can see cars moving along the A591 far below.

Twenty-three years ago I ran up here and thought to myself 'I've arrived' – arrived at a situation in life, living and working in Ambleside, where I could settle. How wrong I was! I hadn't 'dunroamin' yet and there has been much restless moving around in my life since then, although I always return to Ambleside and to places like Loughrigg Fell to 'touch base'. I suppose it could be said that the Lakeland Fells are my spiritual home, and Ambleside is a special place, as is Keswick too – both of them bases for the fells. They are both loaded with life-experiences and memories for me, but of the two I feel a closer allegiance to Ambleside.

I put the schedule back in the bum bag, spin the bag back round and tighten the compression straps. Then I check my watch again: More than one minute has elapsed since I arrived at the summit and I'd better get going. I set off down the main path, then veer off left down a steep bank, then pick up another path heading down towards Red Bank, with High Close youth hostel in view.

Seeing the youth hostel reminds me that I was offered a job there some twenty-six years ago when I applied to work for the YHA in the Lakes. I knew the hostel, having stayed there with friends as a teenager, and it was a good place – well-placed for Langdale and central Lakes, and yet somehow it wasn't quite what I wanted. I chose instead to go for a job at the hostel in Buttermere, which for me was a more romantic and idyllic place. I phoned the warden and arranged to go and stay there over a weekend for an interview.

At the time I was living in a new town in the West Midlands, where I worked as a trainee programmer at a civil service computer centre. I wasn't really cut out for it and I wasn't very good at it. I was a 'square peg' there, and my efforts to force myself into the hole of a desk-bound career just weren't working. I needed to escape to the Lakes for a complete lifestyle change. I'd been doing a bit of running around the streets in the evenings and walking in the Shropshire hills at the weekends. I'd also been reading about fell-running – which seemed to be the perfect expression of vitality, wildness and freedom in a world that was increasingly tamed, controlled and stupefied. I was on a sort of spiritual path that was resolutely set against much of what I found in modern urban society, and key to my journey were the Lakeland fells, and particularly *running* in them.

The interview at Buttermere went well and the warden, Tony Cresswell, offered me a seasonal job to start in early March. At the hostel I'd bought a copy of the Bob Graham Round booklet *42 Peaks* and I read this on the train back to the Midlands. I found it inspiring and I knew that fell-running was going to be a big thing for me. In the booklet there was a black and white photograph of Joss Naylor running across the bouldery ground at Esk Hause during his record-breaking 72-peak round in 1975, and this photo made a great impression on me. He's running in a hunched style, bare-chested and with an intense look in his eye, completely absorbed in his run and at home in the fells – like a wild animal in some other-worldly wild habitat. The photo summed up for me the appeal of fell-running. I photocopied it at the office, blowing it up with increased contrast so that it looked more like a screen print, and then I put it in a clip-frame to hang on the wall as an inspirational image.

And so I moved to Buttermere in March to work as an assistant warden at the hostel, and to throw myself into fell-running. Mornings and evenings were spent working at the hostel, but in the afternoons I would go running on the fells. I would go out every afternoon, whatever the weather, usually on the fell, though in very bad weather or for a rest day I'd run around the lake. I got myself fit and I got myself into places which I couldn't have reached in my limited time had I been walking. I joined the local club, Keswick AC, and did a few races, my first one being the Buttermere Sailbeck, which started and finished in the village. Later in the season I did the Skiddaw and Borrowdale races, but that was all I could do as I had difficulty getting time off at weekends. It didn't bother me too much as I was happy to go running on my own in the afternoons. A few races were good for the social and to have goals to aim for, but it was simply getting out there on the fells that really mattered, and I saw fell-running more as a spiritual activity than as a sport.

The beauty of the Lakeland fells brought out a response in my soul that was more than just an appreciation but an *excitement*. Something about the layout of the land – the ridges and valleys with their lakes, the combination of lush greenery and bare grey crags and the endless variation within such a compact area is special. To walk these fells is not just a pleasure but an inspiration, a communion with natural beauty and wildness. To run the fells is the same, only more intense. Carrying less, moving faster, there is a greater awareness of the immediate surroundings and a greater at-oneness with the fell environment. There's a sense of space, of freedom. You become an animal just doing your thing in your natural habitat, celebrating the self and celebrating the fells in a joyful pagan communion of man and fell. To be fit and running along a lofty ridge, preferably on a summer's day, wearing just a pair of shorts and some studded shoes, the sun high in the sky, the valleys and civilisation far below, is to feel freedom, vitality and joy. It is to be like a feral animal, thankfully released from domestication. And there's a sense of victory in the achievement that is gained by self-direction, self-propulsion and self-rewilding.

A Natural and Meaningful Route

Trotting along the road, past the junction for High Close and Elterwater, I'm wearing a pair of Inov8 Mudclaws – fell-running shoes with sticky rubber-studded soles. I don't like wearing them on tarmac as the studs wear down quickly, but this stretch of road only lasts a couple of hundred yards before I take a narrow path on the left leading up a steep bank through the bracken.

A good pair of shoes is all the equipment you need for fell-running. At one time everyone wore Walshes because they were pretty much the only fell shoes on the market. But when companies such as New Balance, Salomon and Inov8 started to offer an alternative the Walsh monopoly came to an end and most people now wear Inov8s. These days there are so many different shoes to choose from. These Mudclaws are the best for me – giving a good grip on all surfaces, a stable low profile, snug fit and enough cushioning. Most of the time I'm not conscious of them being on my feet – which is a mark of a good pair of shoes.

The path climbs through the bracken, crosses a small stream, goes through a swing-gate, climbs again to another swing-gate, then drops down to a boggy area with stepping stones and a crossroads of paths. I take a direct line to the right of the stepping stones towards a steep craggy bank, and then it's a short scramble up the rocks beside a wall. It's nice to get the hands involved to some degree, although I'm not a rock climber. A bit of scrambling adds some interest, some punctuation to the run. At the top of the rocky section I follow the wall to my right for a couple of hundred yards, then veer off left, over a small stream, then follow a path contouring through the bracken. I get to an area that would make a good wild camping spot, were it not right beside the path. There's a nice flat grassy patch beside a large boulder, and something about the spot just looks good for camping. I'm always looking out for wild camping spots when I'm fell-running, not that I'm thinking of moving out of the wood any time soon.

The route from here to the top of Silver How is very fiddly, with its many twists and turns and ups and downs and, unless you know it really well, it's difficult to get the optimum route – which entails gradually climbing, or holding your contour, but descending as little as possible. I know it well, having run this route countless times on training runs, recces and in the annual Loughrigg-Silver How race, which is a non-calendar event held every February. It has also been run a couple of times in the summer, on the second occasion as an English Championship race.

Continuing upwards, past a ruined building on my left, I make steady progress upwards. For those who are not sure of the route it's very easy to drop too low into juniper bushes in an attempt to approach Silver How directly. But the best line of approach is to keep high to the left, and then swing round to approach a rocky gully. From the top of the gully it's an obvious path all the way to the top of Silver How. I jog a bit and walk a bit and reach the top at 7.27, which means I've run from Loughrigg to here in 36 minutes – four minutes faster than scheduled, so that's good. The next two legs to Blea Rigg and Sergeant Man are the most fiddly route-finding bits in the whole round, but I've recced this bit the most and am confident I know where I'm going, especially in this clear visibility. I can see the peak of Sergeant Man to the north and it doesn't look all that far, but I know from my recces that it's further than it looks, and I've scheduled one hour and five minutes to get there from here.

Running down and contouring round hillocks on a mixture of rocky paths and grass I'm making steady progress in the right direction along this broad ridge between Langdale to my left and Easedale to my right. At one point the path swings a long way to the left to avoid a boggy depression but I carry straight on, veering to the right a little to avoid the worst of the bog, and then climb up the steep bank on the other side. This becomes a rocky path, but I try and stay on the grass, well to the right, as much as possible. And then I contour below the path on a faint trod that cuts out some of the climbing as well as the rocky stuff. I turn round a crag and as I jog up the grass towards a perched boulder my attention is drawn to a small grey bird – a stonechat that flits from one rock to another, making its distinctive call that sounds like two small stones being tapped together. It seems I've disturbed it and it's agitated, or maybe it's just excited and greeting me – the first human of the day to enter its habitat. And then I rejoin the path, which promptly splits, and here I take the right fork which meanders around Little Castle How and Great Castle How, with the 'castle' of Blea Rigg now in view. I trot past a couple of small tarns and some massive boulders before I reach the foot of this, the highest and most impressive of these rock castles. To my left is a gnarled old holly tree growing out of a crevice in the crags, and if I was going to contour around Blea Rigg I would head in that direction. But I'm going to go straight on and climb the stony path to the top of the castle, through the rock battlements and then the final steep climb up the grass to the summit: a cairn atop a rocky bluff. I stop for a moment to take the schedule card from the bum bag and note the time: 7.59am (32 minutes from Silver How).

Blea Rigg is a very characterful fell top with its multitude of rocky outcrops and some small tarns – a fascinating rock 'garden', although the only discernible vegetation is grass, close-cropped by the sheep. I had wondered whether to include this top in the round or whether to bypass it, but decided that it should be in, partly because it's such an interesting top, often overlooked by fell-runners, and partly because to by-pass it would probably only save a few minutes anyway. It's a 'Wainwright', which is to say that it's a top in AW's *The Central Fells* guidebook, and so it is visited by Wainwright-baggers, among others.

I first discovered Wainwright guides as a teenager, when I was first getting into fell-walking. I received them as Christmas presents and read them cover to cover, which fired my imagination for my solo youth-hostelling and fell-walking trips. They were great for route-planning, in conjunction with Ordnance Survey maps, showing all the paths, the ridge routes, the mileage and feet of ascent. The drawings brought the fells alive and showed so much more than the OS maps could. Also the neat handwritten text was full of interesting information, often entertaining with AW's gentle wit. And the guidebooks have been useful in planning this big round, especially for fells like Blea Rigg, where the ground is quite complicated. The distances are in miles and the elevation in feet, which suits me as I am of the age where I think in those terms rather than metres and kilometres. In plotting the mileage and feet of ascent for the route I used a combination of Wainwright guides, OS maps and an old map wheel. Not for me any high-tech GPS gadgetry!

It was in 2009 that I decided to look into plotting my own round, a route that went in a big loop of the fells, but which could be completed in daylight hours. After much poring over maps and planning, the idea of the Freeman Round was born. Less arduous than the Bob Graham Round, the emphasis was on runnability, and also on creating a natural and meaningful route, incorporating sections of a number of classic races (Loughrigg-Silver How, Borrowdale, Anniversary Waltz, Helvellyn, Fairfield), and also most of one section of the BGR. I was looking for a balance between peak-bagging and going for a 'natural' running route. A certain amount of peak-bagging was good, but there should be some peak-*avoidance* in preference for a nice uninterrupted and *enjoyable* line. The original route I had planned was for 50 miles with 25 peaks and 13,500' of ascent and I started recceing the first sections in September '09, but then put it on hold for the winter and then forgot about it for a few years – but then came back to it in the spring of 2013, in my fiftieth year. I began looking at the route again and getting out recceing the sections and trying different permutations of peaks. It was important to me to keep the distance at 50 miles, but the number of peaks was less important. Blea Rigg was in and out of my plans a number of times before I settled on it being in. Green Gable was added, Dale Head was dropped, Maiden Moor dropped, Latrigg added and Low Pike added. Maiden Moor was dropped because I felt it was hardly a top at all and wasn't worth the slight diversion just because it was a 'Wainwright'. Watson's Dodd, on the other hand, although again hardly a top, was included to make up the magic round figure of 50 miles. Dale Head was dropped because I find it such a spirit-sapping trudge from Honister, and also an unpleasant jarring descent down to Dale Head Tarn. I'd heard about the contouring route round the side of Dale Head, as used in the Cumbrian Traverse, and, once discovered, I decided this was definitely the way to go. I ummed and ahhed about High Pike and Low Pike on the descent of Fairfield, but decided to include both since High Pike was en route and Low Pike is a distinctive little top which used to be a checkpoint in the Rydal Round fell race. Latrigg was an additional peak to the original plan, and a worthy addition which bumped up the climb by nearly 1,000'.

The planning of the round became a bit of a numbers game, but eventually was finalised at 50 miles, 28 peaks and nearly 15,000' (The mileage and feet of climb have never been tested by GPS device, so it may be that these figures are inaccurate.) I had a bunch of hand-written spreadsheets listing location, summit number, leg mileage, leg climb, estimated leg time and actual time and used these on my recces. Today I have one in my bum bag on a section of old photo album with a sticky card back and cellophane front – which I peel up to pencil-note my times at each checkpoint. The route on this sheet is divided into four sections: Ambleside to Honister, Honister to Hawse End, Hawse End to Newsham and Newsham to Ambleside. The first and fourth sections are long ones at 18 miles and 17 miles respectively, and the second and third sections are just 6½ and 8½ miles long. Here and now as I stand atop Blea Rigg, the third top of the round, I can see from the sheet that I have covered 2 miles and 950' from Silver How and that it has taken me 32 minutes – which is 3 minutes faster than scheduled. Just another 25 tops, 12,240' and 43 miles to go.

A hundred yards west of the summit of Blea Rigg is the Shelter Stone: two massive boulders joined by a short section of dry stone wall. I've explored this place on my recces and once even considered *living* up here. But as Wainwright noted: 'The accommodation is strictly limited'. The Shelter Stone would provide good protection in bad weather as it's like a little cave inside, with enough room to sit but not enough room to lie down. It could possibly make a 'kitchen', but I'd have to sleep in my tent nearby. A while ago I was offered a job in Grasmere, but there was no accommodation to go with it, or in the village, so I thought maybe I could live up here and commute. It would be a tough commute though, and risky leaving all my stuff on a popular fell-walkers' route – and yet, years ago I worked with a chap at a vegetarian restaurant, 'The Rowan Tree', in Grasmere and he was without a home, so he camped beside Easedale Tarn. He was only there for a few weeks though, before he found a room in Ambleside, and living like that is usually only a temporary thing.

But there have been those who've managed it long-term, such as the famous Millican Dalton who lived in a cave on Castle Crag in Borrowdale for years (although he actually spent the winters at his parental home in London). Also I've heard that a manager of an outdoor shop in Ambleside lives in a tent in some secluded spot on Loughrigg and commutes to work by walking down the fell. Occupying a small room in a house shared with others would feel very claustrophobic after being used to having the fells as your home – the cave or tent as your bedroom, and the Great Outdoors as your living room. 'Great' on a good weather day, but not so great when the weather is bad. I've done it myself, of course – at Rascal How and up Rigg Beck. It's a challenge to live like that, but a worthwhile one perhaps. It's more or less what I'm doing now, although the wood offers more protection from the elements than the open fell.

Going Your Own Way

Leaving Blea Rigg behind I break into a trot and head for the next top: Sergeant Man. After a few minutes I arrive at a boggy area and take a good line, keeping well to the right. And then, after running along the rocky cairned path for a while I veer off to the left on a well-rehearsed grassy contouring route that is more direct than the meandering path. Such a route choice is the stuff of fell-running – where going off the beaten track is about reading the ground in order to get the optimum route. The optimum route is the fastest route. It may also be softer underfoot than the rocky path, though often requires more agility and concentration. When you are following a cairned path you don't have to think too much about where you are going, but when you are off the path and moving relatively fast, you need to be thinking on your feet all the time. This is one of the joys and satisfactions of fell-running – to be working out one's own way rather than following the well-trodden path. And I think this reflects an attitude to life in general: imaginative, adventurous, self-responsible, individual. He or she 'who lets the world, or his own portion of it, choose the plan of life for him, has no need of any faculty than the ape-like one of imitation.' So said JS Mill in *On Liberty*. Fell-running, it seems to me, is essentially about liberty, freedom – and going your own way rather than following a pre-defined path or plan is at the heart of the fell-running mentality. Having said that, most fell races have pretty much pre-defined routes, with just a little scope for variation. And that most famous of big rounds of the fells, the Bob Graham Round, has a pre-defined and very *well-*defined route nowadays, such that no imagination is required – just a high level of fitness and endurance. But before the BGR there were other big rounds...

The first recorded person to complete a big walking round of the Lake District was Samuel Taylor Coleridge in 1802. His 'circumcursion' covered over 100 miles, starting and finishing in Keswick, visiting the Western dales and walking over passes but not actually going on the tops, except for the Scafells. Nevertheless, it was a big journey, travelling light, over 9 days. The idea of walking long-distance rounds of the fells developed later in the nineteenth century, and in 1870 one Thomas Watson covered 48 miles and 10,000 feet of ascent in just under 20 hours in the first recorded version of bagging all the 3,000' peaks in one day. The start and finish point was in Keswick, and this became the norm for 24-hour record feats. In 1902 SB Johnson of Carlisle completed a 70-mile 18,000' round in 22½ hours, and a couple of years later a Dr. Wakefield of Keswick set the record twice, his aim being 'to ascend the greatest possible number of peaks over 2,000 feet, and return to the starting point within twenty-four hours.' These long-distance rounds developed from walks into walk/runs and Wakefield wore lightweight kit (rugby shirt, shorts and gym shoes). The record was improved upon in 1920 when a 54-year old Eustace Thomas (wearing nailed boots) covered 23 tops of Wakefield's route in 21 hours 25 minutes.

In 1932 Bob Graham pushed the tally to 42 peaks in a time of 23 hours, 39 minutes (though including Steel Fell and Calf Crag, which are under 2,000'). The distance and feet of climb were overestimated in subsequent newspaper reports, but the generally accepted figures today are 27,000 feet and 66 miles. Graham's record stood for 28 years until Alan Heaton (inspired to take up the challenge by an article in the Lancashire Evening Post by Harry Griffin) broke it with a time of 22 hours, 18 minutes, following Graham's route, although going anti-clockwise. This route became the established route for the basic 'Bob Graham Round', although further tops were subsequently added by those seeking to improve the '24 Hour Fell Record' and Joss Naylor pushed this record to a remarkable 72 peaks (100 miles, 37,000 feet) in 1975. On June 19th, 1982 Billy Bland set the fastest time for a standard BGR at an incredible 13hrs, 53 minutes.

The booklet *42 Peaks: The Story of the Bob Graham Round* was an early inspiration for me to take up fell-running and having a go at the round one day was something I wanted to do – but there was no rush and

I preferred to race with Ambleside AC or go for runs of up to just a few hours. My longest fell race was the Ennerdale Horseshoe Race in '96 at 23 miles and 7,500 feet and it was over ten years later that I started to think seriously about going further. I started looking closely at the route of the BGR and going for long recce runs. I also helped my old friend Stuart Shuttleworth on his BGR in 2009, supporting him on leg 3 (Dunmail to Wasdale Head). But there came a point where I started to think that it was too much, too far to really enjoy the experience. With my background of years of fell-running I was probably capable of doing it but I think it would have been an ordeal to complete mainly for the satisfaction of completion than for the journey itself. Like many fell-runners I felt almost *obliged* to do the BGR, whether I really wanted to do it or not. The BGR is such a big thing in the history and culture of the sport that to most fell-runners it cannot be ignored. There are those who are quite clear that they don't want to do it – they'd rather focus on racing, and that's fair enough. For myself, I'd always enjoyed the medium horseshoe races most of all, and they were what I did best, but there was something about the big route, of being out on the fells all day, that appealed. I'd never been keen on running on the fells in the dark – having had numerous ankle injuries over the years and not being in possession of a powerful head torch – and that aspect of the BG put me off a bit. I had done some night fell-*walking* but running on the fells was something I only really wanted to do in daylight hours.

It wasn't just that the distance and the feet of ascent of a BGR seemed like too much, but also that it was this clearly defined route that hundreds, if not thousands, of people had trodden before. It was the way that fell-runners aspire to doing this challenge in the same way that road-runners aspire to doing the London Marathon – because it's a famous and legitimised package that can be bagged, something recognisable to put on one's fell-running CV, a rite of passage, a joining of a club.

Rounding a grassy hillock, I rejoin the winding path and the rocky dome of Sergeant Man appears up ahead. I've seen it in the distance, ever since Loughrigg, a prominent object and beacon to aim for, though it is – as Wainwright put it, 'merely a rocky excrescence at the edge of the broad expanse forming the top of High Raise'. The word 'Man' is derived from the word 'maen', which means stone, and the word 'Sergeant' is derived from the Latin *servient*, meaning to serve. Thus Sergeant Man is a subservient stone, or craggy dome, to the master of High Raise, of which it is a secondary summit. It is however a nice little scramble to the top, which is all bare rock, still bearing the scratch marks from the nailed boots of fell-walkers decades ago.

Standing on the top I am the master of all I survey: a panorama of mountains and the broad plateau ridge of High Raise stretching to the north. I still haven't seen another human being since the man in the bowler hat in Ambleside. The time is 8.28am and it's taken me thirty minutes to get here from Blea Rigg.

The distance between the two is only two miles but the way is constantly up and down, twisting and turning. I consider those words 'master' and 'servant' for a moment. Years ago I remember seeing a tattoo on the arm of fell-runner Gary Devine: 'NO MASTERS' I think that at one time he was in an anarcho-punk band, and I think that kind of music goes with the sport. I remember that when I first moved to the Lakes and took up fell-running the music of the Sex Pistols connected in my mind to fell-running. I suppose that both punk and fell-running are about energy, self-reliance, wildness and freedom. The true spirit of both punk and fell-running is to not be a servant to the well-trodden path, but an adventurer on a life less ordinary.

Trotting onwards along a well-trodden path for now, I'm heading for High Raise, and sometimes it makes sense to follow the path – if only to avoid the boggy bits. And it's a straightforward half mile jog, with a stream jump at one point, that takes me just ten minutes to get to the summit, which is known as 'High White Stones' – perhaps so-called because of the whitish algal crusts on the rocks hereabouts. There's a stone wind shelter, a large cairn, a trig point column and an excellent view.

The view from High Raise is all-encompassing, this being Lakeland's most centrally situated fell. Its summit at 2,500' is the highest point on this central north-south ridge which runs from the Langdale Pikes in the south to Bleaberry Fell in the north. Looking south-westwards, which is the direction I'll be taking next, I can see Bowfell, and you can see why it is so-called from here as it actually looks like a bow – as in bow and arrow, or even more like a curly bracket, with the pointy bit on top. To the right is Esk Pike, Scafell Pike, and then Great End. Further round to the west the upthrust 'plug' of Great Gable looks a long way from here, and yet it's the next but one top on my round and less than an hour away. Gable could be considered to be the hub of the Lakeland fells since a number of valleys radiate from it like spokes of a wheel; also it's 450' higher than High Raise and has a much more commanding appearance – a true mountain, as opposed to this featureless grassy moor. But High Raise is definitely worth a visit for the view, and is a necessary part of the route to link up with the next chapter of the journey.

Fell-Dancing

At the trig point I note my time on the schedule card and set off in a south-westerly direction, descending through some boulders to pick up a path that isn't mentioned in Wainwright's guide, but which is marked on the Ordnance Survey maps. I think it's not a very well-used route and the path can be hard to find at first. Basically I am heading for Langdale Combe and Stake Pass, from where I will get onto the ridge that will take me to my next top: Rossett Pike. I locate the nice grassy path and enjoy 'dancing' down the steep slope. Fell-running is a sort of dance, a loose-limbed activity of constantly-changing tempo, as opposed to the stiff and repetitive plod, plod, plod of road-running. The 'fell-dance' exercises the whole body and is a celebration of being physically alive. The 'music' that is danced to is the pumping of the heart, the rhythm of the breathing, the thud and splash of the feet drumming out a beat on the skin of the fell-body. Sometimes there is the accompaniment of the sound of the wind, or skylark-singing or raven-squawking, or perhaps the 'earworm' of some music that was listened to before the run.

Some people like to take their music with them on the run – with an MP3 player or some such. Whilst I can understand this if someone is running along noisy urban roads, I think it's a shame to do it on the fells. For me, fell-running is essentially about a communion with Nature, and to get the best out of that communion all doors of perception, including ears, should be fully open to the experience of the natural environment. Otherwise you might as well be in a sort of outdoor gym. I do think that recorded music can complement the experience, but personally I'd rather listen to music *before* going out running and then have the imprint of it in my mind whilst I'm on the run.

Soon after I started fell-running I got into the habit of playing music before I went for a run, whilst I changed and did a warm-up exercise routine of stretching exercises – if I was running from home that is. Back in the early days the music I would often listen to would be a CD by New Order – *Substance 1987*, or maybe something by Killing Joke such as *Extremities, Dirt and Various Repressed Emotions*. It needed a beat and some sort of hook – a guitar riff, an excerpt of singing, some choice words, a sense of going somewhere, a feeling, a meaning that would stay with me or come back to me on the run – especially when I needed to dig deep and push myself hard up a climb, or maybe whilst running fast along a ridge, or perhaps whilst trying to catch someone in a race. Music can have this magical power to animate and motivate. Everyone has their own tastes and for some it might be Wagner that does the trick, whilst for others it might be electronic trance or heavy metal. Personally, lately I've been getting my inspiration from Iggy Pop and the Stooges, and also a couple of albums by Sonic Youth.

Anyway, I dance downwards into Langdale Combe, changing tempo lower down as the gradient eases, lengthening my stride, jumping over a beck, weaving through the drumlins, climbing up a steep bank, crossing the Stake Pass path and then continuing up the pathless steep slope to get onto the somewhat indistinct ridge that will lead me to Rossett Pike. On one of my recces I dropped down into Langdale Combe in thick mist and completely lost my bearings. It's a confusing area in mist, to be sure. I was off the path and the ground looked unfamiliar. There were large 'erratic' boulders and a lot of boggy ground. I got my map and compass out, but I didn't know how far I'd strayed from the path. I knew I should be heading in a south-westerly, veering westerly, direction and I realised that I must have carried on heading too far south-west and ended up heading for Martcrag Moor. I decided to plough on in this direction until I picked up the path heading south-south-west for the Langdale Pikes and north for Stake Pass. Thereupon I turned right (north) and soon a small tarn appeared up ahead and I knew I was back on track to get onto the ridge leading to Rossett Pike.

Mist can be very disorientating. It's not just that the extent of visibility becomes limited, but also that familiar ground can take on a very unfamiliar look. I carry a map and compass on cloudy days, but if I have to look at the compass I generally only need a rough bearing as I am pretty familiar with the general layout of the land, having spent a lot of time on the fells over the years. I have never been drawn to the micro-navigation of orienteering as for me this would take the fun and the freedom out of fell-running. The ground can be so complicated on the fells anyway that following a precise bearing is not always helpful. Close map-reading and being able to read the ground from experience and instinct is more useful. Going off-course in mist is inevitable to some extent, and it slows things down, but as long as small mistakes are soon corrected then it doesn't become a big problem.

I don't have a map and compass with me today as the sky is clear and the forecast is good. The section now to Rossett Pike is not straightforward, even in clear weather, but I've reccied it enough now to know the best lines. On some of my early recces I had a tendency to contour too far down on the north-west (Langstrath) side of the ridge, but then realised that it's better to follow the line of the ridge as far as possible to Littlegill Head, and then do some fiddly contouring, followed by a steep climb up rocks to the summit. It's a long ridge and at first it takes longer than you'd expect – in fact about 45 minutes from High Raise to the summit. Beyond the notch of Littlegill Head the faint path winds around rocky outcrops and boggy areas, and it's not easy getting the optimum line because the ground is complicated. There are in fact a number of faint paths, which adds to the confusion. The thing to make sure of is that I'm going steadily upwards, rather than just contouring round. The general trend has got to be upwards because there's still a bit of a climb up to Rossett Pike. Sometimes I'm on a faint path and sometimes I'm just making my own way. I can see the top now, and so I need to bear left off the path. You have to work it out for yourself along here. Approaching the rocky top it looks a bit like a Dartmoor tor on a bigger scale, with its clitter of rocks that have rolled down around it. I make my way up through the jumble of big coarse-textured grey boulders, speckled with vivid lime-green lichen. Topping out onto the ridge-crest it's not immediately obvious which is the highest point, but over there is a cairn that marks the summit, and that's my checkpoint, where I stop to note the time: 9.16. It's taken me 41 minutes to get here from High Raise, which is 4 minutes faster than scheduled – so that's progress.

A short distance to the south-east there's another cairn, which marks an excellent viewpoint over the crags which plunge down to the valley of Mickleden. I've been there on previous recces, but today there isn't time – which is a shame because it's a dramatic vantage point. The ground falls away suddenly, and you can see Rossett Gill and the path zig-zagging upwards away from the chasm of the gill. Directly ahead there's the broad gravel-banked Mickleden Beck flowing down the U-shaped valley to the walled green fields of Great Langdale. Lingmoor Fell is in the distance, and beyond Lingmoor you can see the lake of Windermere and the white buildings of the Low Wood Hotel at its shore – some ten miles away as the raven flies. Rising up to the left of Mickleden are the Langdale Pikes, and on the other side, above Rossett

Gill, is Bowfell, its huge sloping slab of Flat Crags catching the sunlight like a giant solar panel or a mirror.

I remember running down Rossett Gill when I was a student, some years before I took up fell-running. I was on a college club trip and a group of us had walked from the Old Dungeon Ghyll via The Band to Bowfell and then descended via Rossett Gill. I remember just breaking into a run because it felt natural and fun. Another lad joined me and we charged down the track in our boots and rucksacks, full of youthful enthusiasm. It wasn't the way a fell-walker is supposed do it – cautious and restrained, but it felt good to take the brakes off and go along with the force of gravity. It was less halting and jarring than walking – more flowing and agile and vital. More *in the moment*, the mind more keenly focussed and the body more keenly engaged with the terrain – running down the stony path, jumping over rocks, scampering down a grassy shortcut, twisting and turning and steadily dropping down into the valley below, it was exhilarating, it was a celebration of being alive – a fell-dance.

The Wilful Freedom-Seeker

And now I trot down the easy path to Rossett Pass, veering off right to Angle Tarn, where I see a couple beside their tent, this being a popular wild camping spot. We wave to each other, and I realise that these are the first people I've seen on the fell today. I step over the huge boulder stepping stones crossing the tarn outlet stream and head up the pitched path, on the way to Sty Head via Esk Hause. I'm on a main highway through the fells, a very well-trodden route that leads to Borrowdale or Wasdale, or any number of the high fells in this area. To my left are the Hanging Knotts of Bowfell, and a little further on is the hulk of Esk Pike, the col of Ore Gap between them. And I think of the Langdale Horseshoe Fell Race, which was never one of my favourites. I remember doing it on a horrible wet day with the cloud down low and not enjoying the Bowfell-Crinkle Crags section, which is rough underfoot. The rocks were greasy-wet and navigation a little tricky, and I was just hanging on as best I could, but losing a few places. Some fell-runners relish the rough stuff, and even the bad weather, but not me. I used to enjoy running on the rocky central fells more in my youth, but after years of ankle injuries and reduced shock-absorbency in my foot pads I don't enjoy it so much anymore. Give me smooth grassy terrain any day. Yet today I'm heading for some of the roughest rocky terrain Lakeland has to offer – on Great Gable, and I couldn't not include this special mountain on my big round. But Gable is over an hour away yet on this section which is the longest one between peaks. And right now I'm power-walking up a well-made rock staircase, on my way to Esk Hause.

Some of these rock staircases pitched paths are clearly useful in combating erosion and canalising fell pedestrians in the way the National Trust wants them to go. From a fell-running point of view they are usually okay for going up, but no good at all for coming down. And even going up they can be tiresome, and an affront to the wilful freedom-seeker who doesn't like to be 'told' where to go and doesn't like to see wildness controlled or tamed, erosion control notwithstanding. Such a free spirit doesn't want to be controlled or tamed himself.

I'm not totally against footpath repair work in the Lake District and some of it is useful and necessary. But I think the 'Fix the Fells' project has gone too far, and teams of volunteers are constructing rock staircases or gravel highways in places where it's not justified. Although they see themselves as 'fixing' the fells, in many cases I think they are damaging them, even *desecrating* them. A certain amount of erosion is natural and inevitable and can be caused by heavy rain as much as by fell-walkers, fell-runners and mountain-bikers. Sometimes ugly scars on the fellside are produced by heavy foot-traffic and a widening of the original path, but some of these Fix the Fells paths are ugly scars in themselves. Perhaps increasingly visitors to the fells expect the experience to be sanitized and risk-free. They don't want to get their feet wet or risk turning an ankle. They want the way ahead to be clearly demarcated so they don't have to think about where they are going.

The rock staircase becomes an ordinary path and levels out at a flattish boggy area. There's a large cairn marking the way and I pause to take a close look at the stones of which it is made: some rounded, some angular, and a mixture of colours – some grey, some green-tinged by algae, some rust-red and some a deep purple-red. I wonder if these are all of the Borrowdale Volcanic Series, and wish I had some more geological knowledge to help me appreciate the variety. When you are moving fast through the fells it's easy to miss some of the interesting details en route. We tend to be looking at the big picture most of the time: the layout of the fells, the crags, tarns, streams and sky, but if you take time to stop and stare at the small-scale stuff it can be fascinating. As William Blake said, there's 'a universe in a grain of sand', and the stones in this cairn are a wealth of diverse shapes, textures and colours, and also a wealth of geological information. Anyway, I'd better keep moving...

The path drops down to a stream, and then it's another rock staircase leading to Esk Hause. On this second climb I veer off left of the path, on the route of an old path which is grassier and more direct. It's a bit of a trudge for five minutes, but then it tops out at a cairn, rejoining the main path, and suddenly there is an amazing view of Gable dead ahead. 'Wow!' I exclaim to myself. Although I've seen the view before it's still awe-inspiring. The massive dome has a strong presence that is inviting and exciting. There is something about this mountain, more than any other in the Lake District that is special. It has some sort of spiritual quality – it's a *sacred* mountain. It may not be as high as the Scafells but it appears to be the master of all fells, the mother of all fells, the hub of the whole glorious Lakeland wheel. It has a strong personality that inspires and demands respect, and it's my next destination on the round.

Onwards I trot, past the stone wall cross of the shelter on my left – and I'm reminded that here or hereabouts is where that photo of Joss Naylor on his 72-peak BGR was taken. That look in his eye which I described as 'intense' is perhaps 'switched off' as much as it is 'switched on'. It's the look of someone who has been momentarily distracted from his focus by the photographer, but who is still utterly absorbed in his mission. I remember reading an interview with Joss in the magazine *Athletics Weekly* way back in the mid-seventies, in which he stated that the secret of his fell-running success was his ability to 'switch off'. I must have only been aged about fourteen at the time and was getting into running cross-country at school, but knew nothing of fell-running. Even so, I remember thinking that it seemed a strange thing to say. Surely you had to be switched *on* rather than off?

He could have simply been talking about switching off from the chronic back pain from which he suffered, though I'd like to think perhaps he was also referring to a trance-like state of total absorption in the activity – a state of mind in which one is both switched-on and switched-off at the same time.

Running now down a winding red gravel path, the chasm of Ruddy Gill is on my right and the towering crags of Great End to my left. The fine red gravel gives way to a rocky made path and I veer off to the left, taking a shortcut on soft boggy grass. And so I make my way, sometimes on the path, sometimes on the grass, Gable looming ever larger straight ahead. I pass Sprinkling Tarn on my right, a favourite spot for wild campers, though there are none there today. The running is a little awkward, a little fiddly, demanding concentration and a felldancer's agility, but before too long I have arrived at Sty Head (9.55am, 45 minutes from Rossett Pike), and I pause at the mountain rescue stretcher box to drink some water and eat a dried fruit 'Trek' bar.

These bars are made of cold-pressed dates and other dried fruits, with oats, soya protein and a few other natural ingredients. The food that I've got for the whole round (not all of which I'm carrying right now) consists of three of these bars, a bag of dried dates, a couple of bananas and a little Kendal Mint Cake. And to drink I've got plain water, blackcurrant squash (with added salt for the prevention of cramp) and a small carton of flavoured soya milk. Nothing high-tech, nothing savoury, and not very much at all compared to what some people consume on ultra-distance rounds. I think that when it comes to food and drink it's very much a case of 'courses for horses'. When Bob Graham did his round he consumed fruit pastilles, boiled eggs, bread and butter, milk, pop and strong tea. Billy Bland favoured malt loaf, date and walnut cake and Mars bars. When I supported Stuart Shuttleworth on his BGR he ate a prodigious quantity of food, including cheese sandwiches, sausages and even mini pork pies, as well as the usual fruit.

One day I was recceing my round and met up with James Byrne and Mark Ruscoe from Ambleside AC, together with Mark's brother, who were doing a Cumbrian Traverse. I knew they were out there on some of the same route as myself and had hoped we'd meet up – which we did here at Sty Head. It was good to have some company and we all went up Gable together and then on to Honister, where they stopped for a big feed, but I only stopped for a couple of minutes before pressing on. I wasn't hungry and I didn't want to lose my momentum, but these lads were going to stop for ten or fifteen minutes for a sit down meal of meat and potato stew prepared by Mark's wife, who was there to meet them. How could anyone run after that? – I thought to myself. But some do, and they did, although they never caught me up on the run to High Spy, Cat Bells and Keswick. I remember looking back from the vicinity of Dalehead Tarn and seeing them in the distance. I was feeling good and moving well. They were probably trying to catch me, and being pursued helped me to put my foot down a bit. I met up with them later at the Oddfellows Arms, which became my traditional place of refreshment on these long recce runs from Ambleside to Keswick. A couple of pints of Jennings Ale consumed after a 27 mile, 8,000' run over the tops from Ambleside was beer well-earned, I reckon.

It's not unknown for some people to consume beer *during* an ultra-distance challenge, and Billy Bland on his record-breaking BGR in 1982, according to Tony Cresswell's report, drank a bottle of Mackeson with a sandwich at Wasdale Head. I think Billy had a belief in magical properties of this milk stout, as I have also read that he drank a can of the stuff shortly before setting off in the Ben Nevis race, which he went on to win in record time. The cans are small and the alcohol content is low (was 3% in those days, lowered to 2.8% nowadays), but even so, this is a strange pre-race or BGR intake by most people's standards. The 'magic' ingredient is probably the milk sugar lactose.

Anyway, the key to eating on the long challenge is, I think, to have just enough, so that you are not weighed down or bloated by food, but just on the edge of being hungry. It's the same with eating before or during a race. Energy is used for the digestion of food and you don't want too much of that energy to be diverted away from the legs. Therefore you want food that is easily digestible, a little at a time, that keeps just enough fuel in the tank. This is what works for me anyway.

The Heart of the Shrine

Re-fuelled, I set off on the steep path up Great Gable, but I soon veer off to the left to take a soft grassy direct route away from the pitched path zig-zag. I'm feeling good in myself – my legs feel strong and my body is happy to 'attack' the challenge of this big climb. I've got a long way to go yet on the round so perhaps I should keep more in reserve. But sometimes moving energetically, although using plenty of energy, also *gives* energy as it somehow nudges the mind-body into another gear – a more fluid, animated and fully-engaged state of being. And so I'm going to go with the flow of how I feel and enjoy being in the here and now of moving quickly, confidently and happily up the sacred mountain.

Perhaps the mountain itself gives me energy, inspiring and exciting me with its strong personality. The effect that it has on me is of a different order to that of say Loughrigg. Gable is much bigger, grander and wilder, of course. Beyond my grassy direct line there's hardly any more grass, just rock and more rock. The pitched path takes another zig-zag, but I carry straight on up a steep natural causeway of scree, rejoining the path higher up. And so I progress upwards, sometimes on the path and sometimes taking a more direct line, sometimes with my head down and my hands on knees, sometimes looking ahead with my arms swinging freely. I pass a few walkers, also on their way up, and we exchange brief greetings. Finally the gradient eases off as the path takes me over the convex curve to the summit plateau and the craggy outcrop of the highest point. There's a final little scramble over the rocks to reach the top, where I touch the cairn and check my watch: 10.27. It's taken me 32 minutes to get here from Sty Head. I slide my bum bag round, take out the schedule card and note my time. I'm gaining time on every section and now I'm 23 minutes up on schedule. I take off my rucksack and delve inside for my mobile phone. There's a signal up here, and so I send a quick text message to my old friend Ben Evans to let him know I'm here already. He's going to meet me at Honister with his girlfriend Christeen for a brief re-fuelling and sock-changing stop. He's got a copy of my schedule and should be there in plenty of time, but at the rate I'm going I might just beat him to it.

I hoist my rucksack back on, spin my bum bag back round and set off again, jogging awkwardly over the stones in a northerly, veering north-easterly direction, following the cairns that mark the way towards Windy Gap. This wilderness of stones and boulders has never been easy to run on, although in my youth when I was more agile I might have skipped over them more gracefully. The first time I came up here I was about eighteen and on a week-long fell-walking and youth-hostelling tour of the Lakes. It was the summer holidays after leaving school and before going away to college. I'd spent the previous night at Black Sail Hut, and then walked up the Tongue to Windy Gap through a dreary thick mist. As I climbed up from Windy Gap, just before the summit plateau I broke through the mist into glorious sunshine and a clear blue sky. Being on this high desert of stones, looking down onto the blankets of white cloud in the valleys had a profound effect on me. It was so beautiful and exciting and I had what I could only describe as a mystical experience of all of life being ordered and interconnected. It was a vision or glimpse of some higher plane of reality, with everything alive and connected by a web of light-energy. I felt so alive and so at one with the landscape.

That experience no doubt played a part in establishing Gable as a special mountain in my mind. Many years later I was to live below it at the head of Ennerdale, whilst wardening Black Sail Youth Hostel. But before that, back in 1989 whilst working at the Longthwaite Youth Hostel in Borrowdale, I would sometimes go fell-running up here, and one hot summer's day run up Gable inspired me to start writing poetry, a fragment of which now comes to me: *This lithe lucid animal dances across the boulder-field, carrying his gift from the noon sun, his power has come, his will be done...* I titled the poem 'Sun King' because the sun was key to the experience, giving life, vitality and animating my inner 'sun king', a sort of fell-running daemon of vitality, strength and wilfulness. The title was also inspired by a song of the same name by the band The Cult on their album *Sonic Temple*, an album I listened to during the summer of '89 and which I'd sometimes play prior to going for a run. Anyway, the idea of the 'sun king' has stayed with me and basically means that feeling of being fit and strong and moving fast among the fells, driven by this inner daemon or god that somehow takes over so that I switch off in one sense but am utterly switched on in another. I become 'one-pointed', totally focussed on the activity, communing with the landscape and fully present in the here and now – no wandering thoughts about the mundanities of day-to-day life, but complete absorption in the 'other-worldly' immediate activity.

When I worked at Longthwaite I developed the idea of fell-running as a spiritual discipline, rather than as a sport. It was a sort of Zen practice or pagan communion that altered consciousness. In some ways it was an escape from the 'real world' of work or relationships or whatever, but it was also a life-affirming activity that strengthened the spirit and also helped with life back in the real world. There is an escape, but also a return, and the fell-inspired sun king *carries back with him into the valley his radiant solar energy*. Nietzsche said something along the lines of 'I love all that is transfiguring – love, music, dancing...' etc., and for me fell-dancing can be a transfiguring experience.

Not so much dancing as staggering over these difficult stones right now, I am twenty-four years older than I was when I worked at Longthwaite and wrote the poem, but I still carry the spirit of the sun king and today, on this special day, I feel his resurgence inside of me. It's a sunny day, not noon yet, the sun still rising and giving me energy, and I feel strong and in control as I make the difficult scramble down the rocks to Windy Gap, whereupon I just keep going, climbing Green Gable to the right of the path on a line that is nicer underfoot and swings round to the summit, where I stop at the cairn to note my time on the schedule card – 10.42, and to take in the view.

Looking back across Stone Cove to the massive Gable Crag, the north face of Great Gable that overlooks Ennerdale, somewhere up there, nestling on a grassy ledge not far below the top is the remains of Moses Rigg's hideaway hut. Moses was a smuggler of whisky and graphite and it's thought that the hut was used as a hidden store on his route between Borrowdale and Wasdale. It was first discovered by climbers in 1889 with the walls still in good condition and the remains of a roof, but one hundred years later was reduced considerably by weathering. It could be reached by a scramble up Central Gulley from the North Traverse and stood with walls five feet high and a flagged floor area of about nine feet by six feet. It was a good hiding place, being virtually impossible to see from either the top of Gable, or from the trod below, it being set back against the rock face. It's unlikely that whisky was actually made there, but perhaps Moses spent an occasional night there. To get to the ledge where it stood would be quite a difficult scramble for the average person, but Moses worked at the Honister Slate Mine and would've been stronger and more agile than your average man on the fells today.

In 2005 a team from *Trail* magazine descended Gable Crag via an indistinct grassy rake and found the hut with its walls still between a metre and two metres tall. They also found a couple of lumps of graphite on a shelf built into one of the walls. As a result of this the ruined hut is now recorded in the Lake District Historic Environment Record, the definitive record of sites of archaeological interest in the National Park.

My gaze swings away from Gable Crag towards Pillar, and it's a great view of Pillar from here, the sunlight catching the ridge at Looking Stead, my eyes drawn upwards to the massive mountain itself and to the stepped outline of the Pillar Rock jutting out on the Ennerdale side. And it's a good view of Ennerdale – a classic U-shaped valley with the High Stile ridge on the other side and the River Liza running down the middle through the forest plantations, on its way to Ennerdale Water, which is just out of sight, obscured by the flank of Pillar. Looking to the right I can see Crummock Water below Melbreak, and a little bit of Buttermere on the other side of Haystacks. But my eyes are drawn back to Ennerdale, and to the speck of Black Sail Hut at the head of the valley, beyond the plantations and at the end of the track – a special place for many, and certainly a special place for me as it was my home and workplace for a long season fifteen years ago.

After my teenaged hostelling trips and visit to Black Sail I thought about working for the YHA as an assistant warden, but it took me a few years to get round to doing it. I thought I wouldn't have the skills required, such as catering for numbers, besides which

I'd got myself stuck in a conventional urban rut of trying to have a career in the civil service and generally settle down. Anyway, the career wasn't meant to be and I escaped to the Lakes to work for the YHA at Buttermere, where I found I could learn catering and all the other skills required as I went along. After Buttermere I did stints at other youth hostels in the Lakes and elsewhere before leaving to do various other jobs, but then returning to the YHA down in Somerset, then at Bellever on Dartmoor. After a winter of caretaking the hostel at Bellever I got the job of warden at Black Sail, which was in some ways a 'dream job', although in those days it was a one-man band, except for a little help in July and August, and I found myself over-worked and not getting onto the fells as much as I would have liked. Anyway, it was a special job and a special place to live.

Years ago I came across the word 'fellender' in a dictionary of Cumbrian dialect. Although I've never heard anyone use this word it means someone who dwells in the fells – at the foot of the fell, the head of the valley, with the fells 'on the doorstep' so to speak. When I was at Buttermere I had the fells on the doorstep and it was great to be able to lace up my Walshes and run from the door, with just a little bit of tarmac before getting onto the fell. Living at Black Sail I was even more of a fellender, being pretty much surrounded by Haystacks, Gable, Kirk Fell, and Pillar, and with no tarmac and no public road for miles. That lack of a road makes the head of the valley especially quiet and with a sense of wildness and remoteness. Skiddaw House, 'back 'o Skidda', claims to be the most remote habitation in England, but Black Sail Hut must come a close second, and it actually feels remoter and wilder, being among bigger mountains and with the shortest way in being over the mountain passes of Scarth Gap from Gatesgarth or Black Sail Pass from Wasdale Head.

I walked over Scarth Gap to Black Sail a couple of years ago with a friend from a city down south. As we dropped down into Ennerdale he commented to me that 'You can never get away from road noise!'. He thought he could hear the background white noise of traffic on tarmac, but what he was actually hearing was the sound of falling water in the becks – a background noise in the fells to which his urban ears were unaccustomed. There at the head of Ennerdale the sound of the water falling on the other side of the valley – in Sail Beck and the other streams cascading down the side of Kirk Fell – was amplified by the amphitheatre of the dalehead.

Being off-grid at Black Sail gave a good feeling of freedom and wildness. As well as there being no public road there was no electricity or any mains utilities. Lighting and cooking were by gas, water was from the beck, and heat and hot water were from the multi-fuel stove. Since my time there the YHA has changed a lot and they have 'improved' the hut with electricity and central heating in the dorms, and also a noisy and smelly diesel generator. But back in the days that I was there it was still quite primitive, though it didn't feel uncomfortable. The whole appeal of Black Sail for the hostellers is that 'away from it all' feeling, combined with the convivial company of fellow fell-walkers who appreciate quietness, remoteness and simple facilities.

As a job, wardening the hut on my own was tough, but it had its compensations of giving me a lot of control over how I ran the place (this being at the back end of the good old days of working for the YHA) and also of being somewhere where I was a fellender who could easily slip into the fells from the front door – and not just the fells but the wildest and grandest part of the whole fellcosm: 'the heart of the shrine' no less.

It's good to make time to stop and stare, to contemplate and reminisce, but I really need to 'git garn' on my journey and so I break into a jog and pick up speed down the easy gradient – running celebratorily, on a song-line, a soul-line, the history of my repeated presence on this territory giving me an energy, a vitality. I swing to the left of the main path to take a quicker contouring route, picking up a narrow grass trod to the left of the crags, and emerging at the cluster of dubs at Gillercombe Head. And from here I continue to keep to the left of the path, picking a good line through the boulders, past some rusty old iron fence posts, climbing steadily as I make my way to the top of Brandreth.

True Adventure

The summit of Brandreth is a bleak desert of stones, the highest point having a cairn with a fence post sticking out the top of it. I reach the cairn at 10.55, which is just thirteen minutes from Green Gable and a full seven minutes faster than scheduled. I find myself checking my watch and schedule again, wondering if the scheduled time is too slow or if I'm running too fast. It doesn't feel like I'm pushing too hard – it feels like I'm running well within myself at a comfortable pace. I worry a little that Ben and Christeen may not get to Honister in time to meet me, but Ben did say that he'd get there with plenty of time to spare.

Onwards to Grey Knotts, following the line of a modern post-and-wire fence, it's an easy trot, the stone desert giving way to soft grass. I pass a tarn, and then it's a little scramble up a rocky tor to the east top, reached at 11.01, a scramble back down, over the fence and then picking up a faint grassy trod that swings left below crags before taking a direct line down to Honister Pass. And it's a jog and a scamper down mainly grass, the trod disappearing so that I have to think on my feet about where I'm going until the buildings at Honister come into view. I run through a boggy bit and my feet get wet but that's not a problem – it keeps them cool. I've not even been aware of how my feet feel until now, which is a good thing.

Down I go, with the road to Buttermere now in view, the first road I've seen since the Red Bank road at High Close. As I drop closer to the big visitor centre car park, which is only a quarter full, I cannot see Ben's blue VW Polo and I start to worry, but then seconds later it pulls in and parks up. And my path now joins up with the quarry road as an orange bus emblazoned with 'Honister' drives past with clouds of diesel fumes, ferrying its cargo of via ferrata or guided tour punters, who are either too lazy or not permitted to walk a quarter of a mile up the track to start their packaged 'adventure', their faces at the windows observing the local wildlife of the lone fell-runner doing his own thing.

'Adventure' is a word you hear a lot in the Lake District these days, and usually it's associated with some sort of business chasing the visitor pound by selling some sort of outdoor activity, be that trail-racing, rock-climbing, abseiling, ghyll-scrambling, mountain-biking, via-ferrataring, 'going ape' and so on. Punters pay a fee to be guided into an experience of so-called 'adventure' that is marketed, packaged, risk-assessed and consumed by the would-be adventurer, who is often seeking a high-adrenaline activity, an activity that provides excitement, but which requires no imagination or initiative. It's part of the consumer society in which we live, where we expect everything to be provided for us in shops, or laid on for us at visitor centres. Cumbria Tourism bosses fear that visitor numbers to the Lake District will dry up unless lots of 'adventure' attractions are laid on for especially younger people to consume. And they do have a point. Many young visitors to the Lake District have been brought up to see the world in all its aspects, including the natural environment, as something to be consumed like a movie or a meal, and their experience is only somehow legitimised if it is paid for at a designated visitor centre or adventure centre or event of some sort. It seems that some people only feel they've had an adventure if they've paid good money for it and been herded into it.

And yet true adventure is surely about taking initiative, taking real risks and taking responsibility. To be adventurous is to be bold and imaginative and to do one's own thing rather than following the crowd. It's about self-reliance and creativity, rather than following in someone else's footsteps. It's about getting off the beaten track and taking a road less travelled, or preferably *un*travelled. It's about autonomy, freedom and *wildness*. A true adventure is about going *into the unknown*, trusting to your instinct that you will find a way. Ultimately it's about a wildness *within*, a wilfulness expressed through the outward adventure.

Visitor centres are tame places which I usually avoid, although last year I had a job at one in Grizedale. There the paying customer (£7 parking for the day) is sold the idea of wildness in an environment that is utterly managed and tamed.

'Mountain-biking trails' are mostly just the fire roads used by vehicles for timber extraction – unless you take The North Face route for an 'adrenaline rush', and the 'forest' is basically just a commercial monoculture plantation of Sitka Spruce. If you are used to living in a large town or city then such a place might appear to be wild, but in reality it is anything but. Visitors are guided onto designated footpaths or biking trails that take them through a man-made environment.

I suppose it's all relative. The Lakeland Fells are not a true wilderness, but at least you have the freedom to wander at will 'above the intake wall' and they are significantly wilder than a forest visitor centre. Of course the fells that we see today are 'man-made' or 'sheep-made'. Hundreds of years ago the Lake District was covered in a natural forest that clothed the fells so that only the high peaks poked out of it. That was the 'original' natural landscape that had evolved over centuries, only to be replaced as the land was gradually cleared and given over to sheep grazing. The landscape of the Lakes that we see today is not really natural, although it seems natural to me because it's what I've grown up with and grown to love. On the continuum of natural and unnatural it's still pretty natural, and more so than the urban sprawl of towns and cities. But what is natural and what is unnatural? Some might say that *everything* is natural – the whole material world with its collective objects and phenomena, including the products of human action and intention such as cars, skyscrapers, televisions, nuclear fission, genetic engineering and mobile phones. But I would disagree with this and define natural as meaning existing in or caused by Nature, not artificial, not cultivated, manufactured or commercialised, but *wild*. To be sure, some things are more wild and natural than others. The 'barren' cleared and grazed fells of the Lake District may not be natural in a purist sense but their uplifting effect on the human spirit is in accord with the spirit of the wild and free.

Natural processes evolve, and in the grand scheme of things it could be argued that human intervention and settlement, particularly sheep farming on the fells, has provided an environment that answers the need for wide open spaces and a sense of freedom for the modern human who predominantly inhabits the hemmed-in urban environment. When man and woman lived in this area five thousand years ago they lived a more natural way of life, a life closer to the natural world, and probably didn't feel the need to seek out that sense of freedom from wide open spaces that we do today. However, the Neolithic stone axe makers that camped out in the Scafell area probably also enjoyed the far-reaching views from the high fells and it seems to be something innate, something *natural* to human nature to appreciate far-reaching views, distant horizons. Such views give a sense of freedom, and the prospect of life beyond one's immediate surroundings. In some respects humans have changed very little over the last five thousand years and there have probably always been those who appreciate the high places and those who prefer the lowlands. Early humans probably had a sensitive appreciation of the landscape around them and their relationship to their environment was not simply one of economic exploitation and struggle but also one in which the beauty of the fells and the views over the valleys had an importance in their own right.

Ben and Christeen are out of the car, they've seen me and are setting up a camping chair with my crate of stuff beside it – just in time. And it's a warm welcome for me from friends who are completely understanding of what I'm doing, Ben himself being someone who has done a number of ultra-distance fell-challenges himself. He used to be a top fell-runner in his twenties, but these days he prefers to walk. He's a very strong walker and has set himself the challenge of walking a book of Wainwrights in a day, one book per year, and so far he's completed the Northerns, Centrals and North-Westerns. It's a worthy challenge which involves a lot of planning and recceing of the optimum route between peaks, and then finally doing the big walk on a good weather mid-summer's day, with a bit of roadside support from Christeen, and perhaps his father Alan joining him for some of the way.

Anyway, Ben didn't get my text message from Gable, being without a signal in Borrowdale, but here he is now, and he and Christeen bid me sit in the chair and ask me what I want in the way of refreshment from my prepared crate. First I change my socks, and then I drink some blackcurrant squash and eat a banana. They ask me how it's going and are pleased for me that it's going well so far. I've known Ben for many years as he used to be a member of Ambleside AC, and I used to share a flat with him in Keswick. He and Christeen run the Rohan shop in Keswick.

He takes some photos of me sitting in the chair and changing my socks. A couple walk past, on their way to the visitor centre, and probably wonder what's going on. I take the flat water bottle and a dried fruit bar from the rucksack and put them in the bum bag, then leave the rucksack in the crate as I won't need to carry it now for the rest of the round. I don't want to stop for long as I don't want to lose my momentum, so after just seven minutes I'm on my feet again and jogging out of the car park, Christeen jogging alongside me as we cross the road and head up the grassy slope of Dale Head to the right of the fence. She just comes a couple of hundred yards up the fell with me, but it's good to have that bit of support and company.

The Flow that Transfigures

The sun is shining, the day is warming up nicely and I've taken off my top, which is always a good feeling on a summer's day. It's good to feel the sun on my bare back and it makes me feel more of an animal, a feral fell-animal enjoying my habitat. The less clothing, the closer the contact between man and fell, the more intimate the communion, the greater the feeling of at-oneness. The sun shines upon me and the sun king is within me as I stride up the turf, my legs feeling strong – *I'm a strong animal with strong legs and strong lungs and a strong mind, and my mind is here and my mind is now and this is it and I'm totally focussed on it and I'm totally alive in it* – as I stride upwards on what is usually a trudge, but which today is a joy, my legs moving rhythmically as I gain ground 'effortlessly'. I'm in a state of flow, and I will go with the flow – the flow that transfigures.

After about ten minutes of climbing alongside the fence I see an old quarry spoil heap on the left, and a faint trod contouring off to the right. This is the route of the Cumbrian Traverse and also the route I decided to take for my round to miss out the summit of Dale Head, thereby reducing the uphill slog from Honister and avoiding the awkward steep descent to Dalehead Tarn. And I definitely made the right decision because this 'shortcut' path is a joy to follow, contouring the side of Dale Head until the view opens up and I can see High Spy ahead and Dalehead Tarn in the hollow below it. The path skirts a small crag on the left and then heads for the tarn. In places the ground is a little boggy but it's mostly good easy running that gives a sense of freedom.

Before reaching Dalehead Tarn I cross over the stream and get onto the path that leads up to High Spy, but before too long I've left the rocky main path and am taking a grassier line I've taken so many times before on this route that forms part of the Anniversary Waltz fell race, and which is on one of my favourite training routes from Little Town (the horseshoe of Hindscarth, Dale Head, High Spy). This climb can be a bit tedious when I'm tired, but today, despite having already covered twenty miles and over 7,000' of climbing, I don't feel tired at all. In fact I feel energised and stronger than ever. I'm moving swiftly and enjoying every minute of it.

At High Spy summit there's an attractive, well-constructed cairn, where I briefly stop to note my time on the schedule: 11.56 (just 36 minutes from Honister, which is 9 minutes faster than scheduled). This is the best time of day – noontide, when the sun is high in the sky and my personal energy level is high. When I used to work at the youth hostels we would work mornings and evenings, finishing our morning shift around noon, which was the time to get out for a run on the fells.

Today, right here and now I'm running on the Skiddaw Slates, of which these North-Western fells are composed, rather than the Borrowdale Volcanic Series of such as Great Gable. The Skiddaw Slate fells, less rugged than the BVS ones, are better 'designed' for fell-running with their long interconnected ridges that are good for horseshoe routes and their easier terrain underfoot. And from here to Hause Gate it's mostly very fast running. I leave the summit of High Spy and head off to the right on a faint contouring grassy trod, then turn left on an even fainter trod to take me past a couple of tiny tarns or 'dubs' – where a view suddenly opens up of Derwentwater and the buildings of Keswick gleaming white in the sun. The trod then rejoins the main path and it's a gentle climb up to the rocky top above Blea Crag, past a small tarn, then a small drop, then a super-fast stretch along Narrow Moor. I feel like I'm flying now along this ridge. The running remains effortless and yet I'm going faster and faster, *feeling the heat, the light and heat of the noonday sun beating down as I'm driving on and digging deep in the light and heat of my inner sun, shining strong.*

Maybe I should slow down a little, but now I get to the shortcut drop through the soft boggy grass, a more direct line away from the path and away from the flat 'summit' of Maiden Moor. I decided against including this top in the round as that would be peak-bagging for the sake of it, the more natural route and race route being this grassy line away from the top, linking up with the main path again for the drop down to Hause Gate. On the drop now, I take little paths through the heather to the right of the main path, dancing this way and that down this very enjoyable descent, with its mixture of heather, grass and a bit of rock. There are quite a number of walkers coming up, this being a popular ridge walk, and some salute me as I speed past.

Hause Gate is the col between the Maiden Moor ridge and Cat Bells. It's also a crossroads, with a path going left for Little Town (which I usually take on my Newlands Round runs) and one going right which drops down to Manesty in Borrowdale. Today I'm going to carry on up Cat Bells, which is always more of a climb than expected and is a 'sting in the tail' of the Anniversary Waltz race. I slow to a walk and just jog the flat sections. There are even more people now, Cat Bells being one of the most popular walks in the area. The name Cat Bells is a corruption of Cat Bields, a bield being a shelter, therefore this was where the wild cats used to live. And before arriving at the summit I pass a craggy area named 'Mart Bield' on the OS map, which suggests that pine martens (now probably extinct in the Lake District) used to live up here too.

At the rocky summit there are lots of people having a rest, admiring the view and taking photos. A group of Japanese people are using 'selfie sticks', and from a distance it looked like they were holding golf clubs in the air. At one time – in the late 18th and early 19th centuries – visitors to the Lake District used to use 'claude glasses' (convex mirrors) to view the land-scape with their backs to it and these selfie sticks are a sort of modern version of that. It's a shame that people can't just take in the view directly, rather than having it mediated through the frame and screen of some sort of device. Photos can be useful and fun, but the best way to perceive the landscape is with the naked eyes, and the best images are those that remain imprinted on the mind, rather than on mirror, paper or screen.

I note my time (12.21) and pass swiftly on, going to the left of the main rocky path with all its walkers toiling upwards, running on grass and climbing down one steep bit to gain a good contouring line. Down, down, past more and more walkers and some discarded orange peel, finally dropping down the very steep grass slope to the road, then it's a short rocky path through some trees to bring me out at the drive to Hawse End Adventure Centre, where Ben and Christeen are parked and with the camping chair and crate awaiting my arrival.

Their smiling faces greet me and they congratulate me on my good progress, then it's a quick sit down for another change of socks and also shoes this time – into my trail shoes for the next section, which is mostly hard-packed stony trails. I also put on my turquoisey-blue tech tee-shirt, have a drink of blackcurrant squash and eat a banana. That last section was exhilarating, but I've still got a long way to go and am just about halfway round here. It's good to have a sit down for a little while, but not for too long, and after eleven minutes I'm on my feet again and jogging along the stony path across a field.

The trail shoes have more cushioning than the fell shoes, but the hardness of this ground is hard on the legs and the feet after the soft ground of the fell. The chunky hardcore type of gravel makes a solid path, resistant to erosion, but I can feel those angular hard stones pressing through the rubber soles of my shoes. The path winds through some pleasant mixed woodland and I encounter quite a few walkers as I go. I run past the entrance to the Lingholm Estate and on to Nichol End Marina, emerging at the road and turning right for Portinscale, running on tarmac now, which is easier on the feet than the hard-core stones, but which still has a deadening effect on the legs and the spirit. I'm back in 'civilisation' now, with people and dogs and motor traffic and the sound of a chainsaw. And I think of those words of ST Coleridge: 'The farther I ascend from animated nature, from men and cattle, and from the common birds of the wood, and fields, the greater becomes in me the intensity of the feeling of life.' And conversely, having descended from the fellcosm, I feel within me a loss of vitality. But then I turn a bend in the road and see a fantastic view of Skiddaw dead ahead – massive, graceful, flanked symmetrically by Little Man on the right and Carl Side on the left – and I feel my spirit lifted.

Past the café on the left I turn right to go past the Derwentwater Hotel and then over the River Derwent on the footbridge – the suspension bridge that bounces up and down slightly as I jog over it. Then it's along the wide track across the fields which finally brings me out at Greta Bridge – and now I'm in Keswick, on Main Street, and I'm definitely back in civilisation, among the hustle and bustle of the getting and spending crowd.

Right to Roam

In Keswick pretty much everything is geared to the tourist economy, which revolves around fell-walking, eating, drinking and shopping for outdoor gear. It's also become a very dog-friendly town and many visitors come here with their four-legged friends, which is fine if you're a 'dog-lover', but not so great if you're not. I have lived here, or nearby, at times over the years and I have mixed feelings about the place. On the one hand it's a 'romantic' place, full of character, in a beautiful location and a great base for the fells. On the other hand it's so busy, nay *crowded*, with visitors pretty much all year round now, there are few ordinary shops to meet the needs of locals, rented accommodation is very expensive and the whole culture of the place revolves around making money out of the visitors one way or another. For business owners it's a lucrative place to trade, but where their minimum wage-slaves cannot afford to live, so mostly travel in from West Cumbria. In the twenty-five years or so I've known the town it's changed a lot. It's lost some character, lost some good useful shops and become increasingly a gaudy resort. Like Ambleside it doesn't feel so much like a real community anymore, but more a giant cash register.

And yet part of me still loves it, and I sometimes think I'd like to return to live here at some point, if I can find a way.

Running up Main Street I pass the Co-op on my left, then Bookends bookshop – where manager Janet is outside and waves to me, then turn left up Stanger Street, past the B&Bs, and then right at the top and down to the River Greta and over the footbridge into Fitz Park. Now I have a good view of Skiddaw again, and also of its little wooded outlier, Latrigg – which is my next fell on the round. I jog over the grass to a path that takes me to an iron swing-gate and then I'm on the Brundholme Road for a few hundred yards before turning left up Spooney Green Lane, over the bridge across the A66, and then the steep climb up the broad track through the trees. My legs feel a bit tired as I slow to a walk up the steep slope, and listen to the loud roar of traffic on the road. A view of Skiddaw appears between the trees on my left, and it's one of my favourites for running on, despite the gravel track most of the way up the 'tourist route'. It's certainly a popular one with tourists, as is Latrigg, although the path I'm going to take up Latrigg is not popular, but one used mainly by fell-runners who are familiar with the route from the Latrigg Race. I look out for an old stone gatepost on my right, which marks the start of an indistinct path that leaves the main track and climbs steeply through the trees. Up here I go, and it's a narrow path on grass and earth, climbing steeper and steeper, over tree roots and some fallen trunks – and my legs do feel weary and I'm sweating profusely and feeling a bit dizzy. I wonder if it has something to do with over-consumption of salt in the squash I drank at Hawse End.

I vaguely remember charging down through these trees in the Latrigg Fell race ten years ago, when I was in the prime of my fitness at the age of forty. I finished 8th overall and the first Vet40, which earned me a silver cup engraved with the names of previous first veterans, and including such greats as Billy Bland and Kenny Stuart. But right now I don't feel like a winner, or even a fell-runner anymore. It's come on quite suddenly but I really don't feel good at all. I stop for a moment, slide my bumbag round, take out the flat water bottle and have a drink. There's nothing to do but plough on and hope that this is just a bad patch that I can work through. It would be good to have some moral support, some companionship, and I look forward to seeing Jim a few miles further on. I put the water bottle back and carry on climbing. There's a coniferous plantation on my right now, the ubiquitous Sitka spruce planted in straight lines, which is a dispiriting sight. Finally the slope levels out at a lovely flat area with mature deciduous trees and a patch of green grass that would make a good campsite, were it not for the fact that it's right beside the path, and also that you can still hear the roar of traffic on the A66 up here. The path crosses a track and leads up to a fence with a metal gate which is padlocked, as usual, but it's no problem to climb over it. The fact that it's locked reminds me that this is not a public footpath, but a permissive path through land that is presumably private.

There was some dispute over public footpaths on Latrigg towards the end of the nineteenth century, when the landowner obstructed paths that had been used for years. Members of the Keswick and District Footpath Preservation Society organised a mass trespass in 1887, when 2,000 people marched to the top of Latrigg, removing obstructions as they went. After a court case a compromise was reached and a route up Spooney Green was conceded for public use. It was a victory for freedom to roam on the fells and open spaces which prefigured the setting up of the Lake District Defence Society 'to protect the Lake District from those injurious encroachments upon its scenery which are from time to time attempted for purely commercial or speculative motives, without regard to its claim as a national recreation ground.' As well as fighting to keep footpaths open to the public, the society also fought the construction of a railway in Ennerdale, the extension of the Kendal-Windermere line to Ambleside, a dam on the River Duddon and other threats to scenery and freedom. Later, in January 1895, the work of the Defence Society was taken over by the newly-born National Trust.

Now that I'm over the metal gate I'm on the open fell and climbing a steep grassy path between walls of bracken. I'm starting to feel better in myself just by getting out of the woods into the open air. These slopes used to be wooded all the way to the top at one time, and I see the occasional old tree stump poking out of the grass as I climb this last bit towards a wooden bench up ahead.

At the bench, which is just a little way short of the top, I stop and turn around to take in the view: The town of Keswick is at my feet, its grey stone buildings looking white in the sun. Derwentwater, with its numerous islands, stretches south into Borrowdale. And there's a panorama of fells from whence I've come – the ridge of Cat Bells, Maiden Moor, High Spy, and Great Gable poking out proudly in the distance. And behind Cat Bells, the Newlands fells – like an encampment of giants' tents, as Coleridge described them. It's a beautiful view from here, and one which lifts my spirits some more. I'm more than halfway round now. I turn and trot along the causewayed gravel path leading to the highest point, which is a rocky noddle amid the lush green sward. Again I stop, this time to note my time on the schedule: 13.57.

And then away I go, through a wooden gate and down along the east ridge, a beautiful descent on soft grass at just the right gradient – and I'm feeling better in myself now. I can 'open' my legs here and feel a sense of freedom in my running again. I'm not going to race down here, I need to hold back a bit, but I'm going to let gravity do its work and stay loose in my legs, rather than 'put the brakes on'. The annual Round Latrigg Race comes this way and I used to do well at this one, the fast smooth trail-type running suiting my strengths as a competitive runner, if not satisfying my soul as much as a longer, higher and wilder route. Back in 2003 I was chasing after Alan Bowness down here, not just going with gravity but pushing hard all the way down and then back to Fitz

Park in Keswick along the old railway path – to finish second, which was one of my best ever fell race results. Happy memories, and I know I'll never do that well again. I'm getting older and slower, but when it comes to *endurance* over a longer route such as today's round, I might just be coming into my own.

Down below to my right is the River Greta meandering through Brundholme Woods, and ahead, in the distance, is the big whaleback lump of Clough Head – my next top. The grass path joins with a recently-renovated gravel path, which is uncomfortable to run on. I stop to pick up a piece of the blueish-grey stone: angular, a sharp-edged, quartz-veined nasty bit of hardcore stone – the sort of stone that can do you an injury if it presses through your soft soles and into your feet at just the wrong place. I wonder if this is Shap blue granite. Anyway, I revert to the soft green grass – the skin and flesh, rather than the bones, if you will. I drop down to a gate and a stile and a wooden signpost saying 'Skiddaw 4 miles' pointing in the way I've just come, and I turn left onto a tarmacked lane, which is harder than the grass but more pleasant to run on than the gravel. The lane meanders downhill and at the bottom I go through a gate to join the old railway line footpath opposite an old 'railway man's hut', which is now a visitors' information point.

These information points are a good idea for the visitor who wants to learn something of the history of the old railway and the wildlife in this area. Such information helps you to appreciate the environment more, and I have previously looked at the info boards in this hut, and also in the next one along the line. The huts were used by railway workers – as shelters I suppose, and perhaps also as tool stores. They even had fireplaces, and they would have been cosy places to shelter from the elements and brew up some tea and have a lunch break. The railway line was constructed by navvies using manual tools and gunpowder to blast through rock in some places. It opened in 1864, being part of the Penrith to Cockermouth line, and was used at first mainly as a link between the coalfields of South Durham and the iron-producing West Cumberland. It also carried granite from Threlkeld, lead from Troutbeck, limestone from Blencow and slate from Honister. A few years after it opened it was also carrying thousands of tourists to Keswick, and in 1869 the massive Keswick Hotel opened. As time went by the line became less used for coal and iron ore and more dependent on tourism, but as more tourists started to arrive by road the railway declined and it was finally closed in 1972.

Running now along the line towards Threlkeld I cross over the River Greta on an iron girder bowstring bridge, and then go through a cutting of bare rock festooned with moss and ferns. After the cutting I look over to my left to the river with its steep bank and mature trees clinging on precariously. The water looks green from the trees, but it's actually clear and unpolluted, and is home to otters, trout, salmon and eels. Sometimes you might see a heron perched on a rock and looking into the water for fish. There are also kingfishers, dippers, woodpeckers and wagtails – and it's good to be in an environment where there's plenty of wildlife, although the running experience feels far from wild. The dead flat railway line with its hard stones underfoot is deadening to both legs and spirit, and perhaps a better way to travel along here is on a bicycle.

After about a mile on the line I turn off right on a path up a bank, which then follows the line of the river beneath a concrete flyover carrying the A66. The flyover looks out of place here in the National Park, an ugly structure of a type that could be anywhere, although if it was in a more urban setting it would probably have some graffiti on it. I suppose graffiti artists don't tend to come to places like this, and the whole thing is as unblemished as the day it was built sometime in the early '70s. I suppose that in many ways the A66 was the replacement for the old railway line, a link this time to the M6 motorway, constructed mainly for industrial West Cumbria, and partly for the tourist economy. It's a shame it wasn't routed to the north of the National Park, although it is a useful high-speed link for workers in Keswick who live either in West Cumbria or Penrith.

I come to a road, turn left, go over a bridge then turn right – back onto the course of the old railway line, a tree-lined embankment that takes me to a gate at another road, the St. John's in the Vale road. Just as I arrive at the gate I see Jim's car pull up, and Jim in the passenger seat looking at an OS map. This is a surprise and a worry because he's supposed to be at Newsham to meet me, and that's only ten minutes' run away. I shout and wave, he sees me, gets out of the car and explains that he doesn't know how to get to where he's supposed to be. Karen, his wife, waves to me from the driver's seat. It's very lucky I just happened to come across them, and I'm a bit concerned that he's late, but the only thing to do now is for him to put on his running shoes here and follow me up the line to Newsham. He needs just a bit of time to lace up his shoes and make sure he's got everything he needs in his rucksack so I say 'catch me up' and set off over the road into the little car park and back along the railway line.

This section has a completely different character to the previous section along the Greta. It's not part of the designated railway footpath/cycle track between Keswick and Threlkeld and isn't on the tourist trail. It feels industrial – with a high barbed wire fence on my right, on the other side of which is some sort of goods yard. And beyond that it's just an ugly, unkempt disused railway line in a cutting that could be anywhere in Britain, were it not for the great view of Blencathra to my left. On my right is some sort of factory or industrial units that are part of Threlkeld Business Park. And all this has a deadening effect. Oh well, it only lasts five minutes... I go through a gate and look back to see Jim following on behind, and hopefully catching me up.

Finally I turn off the railway line onto a narrow tarmacked lane that goes over a bridge and there ahead of me is the mass of Clough Head. The lane climbs steadily towards the house called Newsham – and what a great place to live this would be for someone like myself: a true fellender's abode, completely detached, a long way from neighbours and right at the foot of the fell. Ben's blue VW Polo is at the road end, and there's Ben (without Christeen this time) standing beside it. Jim still hasn't caught me up but when I look back he's only fifty yards behind. I'm ready for a break here – a sit down, some food and drink, a change of shoes and a bit of crack with Ben and Jim. The time is 14.16.

And so I sit down in the camping chair and have a look in the crate to see what I should have. I decide on a Trek bar and a carton of banana-flavoured soya milk. I also change back into my fell shoes and a different tee-shirt, then spend a bit of time sorting out the contents of my running rucksack, which will contain Jim's stuff as well as mine, and which Jim will be carrying from now on. Ben asks me how it's going and takes some photographs. He also chats to Jim, who he knows slightly from when Jim and Karen used to run a record shop in Kendal. Then at 14.45, after a long break of nineteen minutes, Ben wishes us well and takes another photo as Jim and I go through the fell gate and set off across Threlkeld Common towards Clough Head.

Back in the Fellcosm

Running together across tussocky grass, reeds and boggy ground I'm reminded of the Helvellyn and the Dodds fell race which I ran a month ago, and which more or less follows the route we're taking today as far as Helvellyn, but then goes back the same way to Threlkeld Cricket Club. I like 'out and back' races, where you can see the leaders on the way down as you're on the way up, and then pass others on the way up as you're on the way down. You can shout words of encouragement to your fellow fell-runners and see how far ahead or behind others you are. There's a lot of fast running in that race, and you have to be careful not to go too fast in the first half out to Helvellyn because it's a long way (7½ miles) back to the start, and although there's less climbing on the way back there's still a lot to do. Overall I had a good race, but my legs 'died' on the final climb up Clough Head and then turned to jelly on the steep final descent, but I managed to keep it going and push all the way across Threlkeld Common and along the final road section to finish in about 2hrs 45mins in 18th position and 2nd Vet50. And then afterwards there was the sitting on the grass in the sun, the beer-drinking, cake-eating and socialising.

The route we're taking now is also basically the second leg of a clockwise Bob Graham Round, although of course from Fairfield we'll be carrying on south to Ambleside, rather than turning west to Seat Sandal and Dunmail Raise. Any round of the central Lake District has pretty much got to include the Helvellyn range, this long north-south high-level ridge. What possible alternatives could there be to link north with south? I could have opted for the High Street range from Pooley Bridge, then Stony Cove Pike, Kirkstone Pass, Red Screes and then that fantastic descent down the ridge into Ambleside. But that would have entailed a contrived route on many miles of tarmac between Threlkeld and Pooley Bridge and added too much distance and taken me too far away from the central Lake District. The other potential north-south link would be the ridge running from Bleaberry Fell in the north to High Raise in the south, but that ridge is mostly boggy and dreary, besides which it would be too short, and wouldn't link up with Ambleside as well to form a complete loop. So the Helvellyn ridge it had to be – no question really.

The origins of my thinking about doing a big round of the Lakeland fells go back to my teenage years, when I was first discovering fell-walking and had a one inch to the mile Ordnance Survey Tourist Map of the Lake District on my bedroom wall. That map was a great picture of the whole of the National Park. All the higher ground was represented in yellow, as opposed to the green of the lower ground in the valleys, and the shapes of the fells were picked out nicely by brown shading on the southern and western slopes. The map was a work of art that made a good picture on the wall, and you still see them on the walls of youth hostels, hotels, shops and offices in the Lake District. A framed one fetches a high price nowadays, as they became a rarity when the Ordnance Survey stopped making them (at some point in the nineties, I think). I still have a folded copy, which I sometimes refer to when I want to see the whole area on one sheet.

The map shows the Lake District as being roughly circular, but split down the middle by the north-south geological fault-line and the A591 running between Ambleside and Keswick. The blue-coloured lakes radiate out from a central point, which is Grasmere, or thereabouts, and there's a symmetry, an order and something special about the layout of the land that suggests a self-contained world unto itself. At one time, when I was dabbling with painting, I had this idea to paint a large square abstract picture based on the one-inch map. I never got around to it, but maybe I will one day. Anyway, the map itself is a sort of mandala – a cosmic diagram representing my own world: the whole of the Lake District, my favourite universe in the whole multiverse.

Jim and I run close together and it's good to have his company. I first met him ten years ago when I was working at Pete Bland Sports in Kendal and he came in to buy a pair of fell shoes. He and his partner Karen had Circa Records in Kendal, and I would sometimes pop in there to browse through the CDs. It was a brave move setting up a record shop in the days of the rise of Amazon, the business proved to be unviable and so after a few years they jacked it in and both went to work at a bookshop. As well as the day job at the bookshop Jim played in a band called The Seven Seals, an indie rock band with a big following in Kendal and beyond. He also works as a self-employed illustrator, and he did the art work for the cover of my novel *The Purple House*. He's a creative man of many talents, now living in Ambleside and making fell-running an increasingly important part of his life.

I'm leading the way because I want to set the pace, and also because I know the way better than Jim, having reccied it numerous times. But we run close together so that we can chat as we run – about fell-running, music, books, jobs or whatever. I navigate us away from the boggy stuff towards the fence over on the right, then we follow the line of the fence for a while, then head towards an old railway waggon with its rusty iron frame and rotten timbers. It seems an incongruous thing here on the fell, but we are not far from the old railway, and also close to the Old Coach Road, which we soon cross, and then we look for the crossing point over the barbed wire fence on the other side. There's no stile (though I think there was one once), but someone has covered the top barbed strand with a section of plastic pipe, secured with tape, and there's a log stump on this side to step onto and enable the crossing. I wonder whether it was the farmer or a Bob Graham contender who modified the fence in this way. Anyway, whoever it was, it was a good idea, making the fence crossing easier and safer. Barbed wire fences can cause nasty injuries and in many places they are completely unnecessary. They are aggressive barriers which don't help relations between the farming community and those wishing to enjoy a wander in the Park, especially when there is no stile provided at a place that needs one.

Once over the fence we have the steep climb of Clough Head ahead of us, and it's the biggest climb in the whole round at around 1,900 feet and with an estimated leg time of 45 minutes from Newsham. It's always a trudge, never a pleasure, going up here. There's a faint trod made by fell-runners heading up the steep tussocky grass and we follow this at a walk. It'll be a walk all the way to the top, an unremittingly steep climb that is out of the sun, being north-facing, and which has nothing to commend it except that it's the most direct and quickest way up. And I think to myself that if I didn't have Jim with me this leg would be very dispiriting.

On the way up we cross a couple of contouring reed-covered old quarrying tracks. We're heading for a gap between two craggy areas on the skyline, to the left of Red Screes, but it'll take us a while to get there. There's no hurry and we have to conserve energy. Also that soya milk I consumed at Newsham seems to be sitting heavily on my stomach and slowing me down slightly. One leg in front of the other, climbing steadily, we eventually gain the top of the ridge and we're back in the sun, back in the fellcosm.

It's a short jog to the trig point, where we pause to note our time, Jim this time in possession of the schedule card. He delves in the rucksack for it, then struggles to extricate it from the waterproof plastic case, finally noting the time: 15.20 (exactly 45 minutes from Newsham, which is the estimated leg time). It's good to have far-reaching views again. Over to the west are the Newlands Fells, then further south there is Gable and the Scafells. Further south-west we can see the Coniston Fells, and in the far distance the glinting sea in Morecambe Bay. Coleridge, in a letter to William Godwin, described the view from his home at Greta Hall in Keswick: '...if impressions and ideas *constitute* our being, I shall have a tendency to become a god, so sublime and beautiful will be the series of my visual existence.' And running around the fells on a clear sunny day such as this, with its ever-changing series of sublime and beautiful views, one can start to feel superhuman. But we must not dwell on this view for too long because we have to keep moving.

Opening the Doors of Perception

And so we set off running down the broad grassy ridge towards the rocky knobble of Calfhow Pike, almost a mile away to the south – and this is nice easy running, and *fast* running, if we were racing, which of course we're not. Looking westwards to the Newlands Fells, from whence I've journeyed, I think to myself – that's where the excitement is. Those are my favourite fells, whilst where I am now is relatively dull, being grassy moorland in character, although giving a sense of airy spaciousness – and it's good to be back on the high fells again after that trail section from Hawse End to Newsham. We can lengthen our stride and feel the freedom of the fells here. And as we approach Calfhow Pike we veer off to the left onto a path that curves round to the east and climbs up to Great Dodd, the high northerly point of the Helvellyn range.

We reach Great Dodd at 15.45, 25 minutes from Clough Head, and Jim struggles with the schedule card again, so I jog on and wait for him to catch me. I don't want to waste too much time hanging around the summits. I'm still up on schedule and want to keep it that way. The next top is Watson's Dodd, which is just a ¾ mile easy jog.

Watson's Dodd is hardly a 'top' at all from here, but rather a flat grassy triangular shoulder that juts westwards from the main ridge. The elevation gain is so minimal that it's hard to see why it's classed as a summit in its own right, and why it's a 'Wainwright', but from down in St. John's in the Vale it presents a more distinctive fell-profile, bounded by Mill Gill and Stannah Gill, and incorporating the impressive Castle Rock of Triermain. It's one of the 42 peaks of the Bob Graham Round, but is by-passed by the Helvellyn and the Dodds race. When I was planning the route of my round I wasn't going to include it because it seemed like 'peak'-bagging for the sake of it, and it seemed more natural to follow the line directly to Stybarrow Dodd, as in the race. However, I decided to include it in the end, purely for the little bit of extra mileage to make the total distance a round 50 miles. And today I'm glad that I included it because it does also give an excellent view westwards: an extensive fell-panorama stretching from Blencathra in the north to the Coniston fells in the south. My eyes are especially drawn south-west to Pillar, Gable and the Scafells.

The time duly noted on the schedule card, we turn south-east for some lovely easy flat running towards Stybarrow Dodd. And then it's a gentle climb up the path, then diverting off left to gain the summit, with its large cairn. It's four o' clock, the sun is shining, I'm feeling good in myself again and still gaining slightly on the schedule. From the top of Stybarrow we take a direct line for Sticks Pass, jogging down through the soft tussocky grass. This route over the Dodds is something of a roller-coaster, and the next climb ahead of us is Raise. At Sticks Pass we join a hard made path which is uncomfortable for the feet after the soft grass, but soon we are on a more natural path through the rocks – and Raise is like a rugged island rearing up from the sea of grass. On close inspection the rock looks volcanic – pitted like pumice stone in places, and from here onwards the ground beneath our feet is rockier and of the Borrowdale Volcanic Series. We reach the top 14 minutes after Stybarrow, and it's easy to knock off these tops, one after another in quick succession. Next up is Whiteside, just another ¼ mile and ten minutes away.

After descending Whiteside the path climbs up the fairly sharp ridge towards Helvellyn Lower Man, and the fell-architecture starts to get more interesting. We can see Helvellyn over to the left, with the ridges of Swirral Edge and Striding Edge dropping away steeply. And it's a steep pull up to the summit of the Lower Man, a distinctive subsidiary top to the main Man of Helvellyn itself. Jim is still struggling to quickly extricate the schedule card, note the time and then put it back in the rucksack, so I jog on ahead towards Helvellyn, leaving him some distance behind. It's just a short jog up quite a shallow slope to the summit, which I reach at 16.22. I shout out the time to him from the trig point, and stop to delve into my bum bag for my mobile phone. I know that there's a signal here and I want to phone Rob Sparkes, who will be meeting us to take some photos on the final descent off Low Pike into Ambleside. He'll still be at work in the outdoor shop so he doesn't pick up, but I leave him a message to let him know that we're running some 45 minutes ahead of schedule. Jim jogs up to join me and I suggest that I take over the timekeeping to save time, and he hands me the schedule card. It's in an Ortlieb waterproof document bag and the prising apart of the opening, the two sides of that transparent material sticking together, is a little difficult if you're not used to it. I can keep it in my bum bag as I did on the earlier sections of the round, and it's quicker and easier for me to do this than to have Jim delve into the rucksack for it. Minutes saved here and there add up, and I might as well try to do the round as fast as I can since I'm feeling good and enjoying it.

Not that there's no time to stop and stare and appreciate the far-reaching views. Helvellyn is a high point, and the highest point on the whole round at 3,118'. I have less affection for it than Great Gable, but it still features in my 'song-lines', my soul-lines as a fell oft-visited over the years on my fell-running jaunts. When I was a regular on Ambleside AC training runs in the nineties we would sometimes run up here from the Travellers Rest Inn, Grasmere. We'd go up Tongue Gill to Grisedale Tarn, and then up Dollywaggon Pike and on to Helvellyn, then back the same way. That would've been a Sunday morning run, or possibly a Tuesday evening one in mid-summer, followed by pints at the Travellers. One summer Saturday a group of us ran all the way from Threlkeld to Ambleside over the Dodds, Helvellyn and Fairfield – a route which I'm repeating today.

Wainwright notes that 'there is no doubt that Helvellyn is climbed more often than any other mountain in Lakeland' and that may be so, though I wonder if Scafell Pike may have overtaken it nowadays. Anyway, there are nearly always people up here, and today is no exception, even though it is fairly late in the afternoon for most folk. But people do come up here at all times of day, and some camp out here overnight to see the sunrise in the morning. The route from the west side is relatively easy, such that many people come up this way who are not regular fell-walkers to bag a peak that is well-known. The very name 'Helvellyn' is appealing in itself, a poetic Cumbric word suggestive of the sublime, the other-worldly, and possibly a hellishness if the weather is bad or the mountain is in a bad mood.

The mountain was well-loved by Wordsworth, who often walked up here, and who described the sublime spell of the mountain working on a friend (a Miss Blackett, who in 1816 was staying nearby) in his poem *To – on Her First Ascent to the Summit of Helvellyn*: 'Thou has clomb aloft, and gazed / From the watch-towers of Helvellyn; / Awed, delighted, and amazed! / For the power of hills is on thee, / As was witnessed through thine eye...' For Wordsworth, Helvellyn was among the grandest of those sublime forms which had a profound effect on his inner life. But the sublime doesn't exist in isolation – it requires an active, participating observer. As Wordsworth put it: 'Minds that have nothing to confer find little to perceive.'

John Ruskin said: 'The greatest thing a human soul ever does in this world is to see something, and tell what it saw in a plain way. Hundreds of people can talk for one who can think, but thousands can think for one who can see. To see clearly is poetry, prophesy, and religion – all in one.' The ability to see clearly is a gift, but also something that can be worked on, I think. Fell-running can open the doors of perception as absorption in the activity takes one away from the preoccupations of everyday mind into the realms of wild mind. But sometimes there is a need for *applied* perception if one is to fully appreciate one's surroundings. By this I mean looking at the fellscape with an artist's or poet's eye, whether or not you consider yourself to be either. There are practical tools which can help: a sketchbook, or a dictaphone perhaps. I have occasionally carried a small tape recorder into the fells and found it to be a useful oral notebook or sketchbook. When I see something that grabs me I speak into the machine, my thoughts are recorded in the moment, and it forces me to find the words to describe the experience. It may be halting, like a pencil and paper sketching, but a picture spun by words is expressed. Sometimes there is nothing much to say, but it's worth remembering that – to paraphrase the 14th century physician, astronomer and clockmaker John de Dondis – we are placed among wonders, and whatever natural object to which the eye is drawn is wonderful, if only we examine it for a while. That is true wherever we find ourselves, but in an area of spectacular natural beauty such as the Lake District you don't have to look very far for wonders. The soul is nurtured by beauty and, as Thomas Moore said, 'What food is to the body, arresting, complex, and pleasing images are to the soul.'

Traversing Helvellyn on the north-south axis is not the best way to fully appreciate its grandeur, which is better comprehended by an eastern approach up Striding Edge, for instance. Looking over the precipice to Red Tarn below gives a sense of excitement and reminds me that I'm now on a proper mountain, not just a tame roller-coaster ridge. And as we jog southwards the rock scenery of the crags on the rugged eastern slopes is impressive. Precipitous cliffs fall away into Nethermost Cove, perhaps the lowest and deepest of the series of eastern coves from Keppel in the north to Cock in the south. It's a long way down into a helvellish nether region. I don't have a dictaphone with me today, but really all you need to do is to keep your eyes open. Also it's helpful to have a sympathetic companion to whom one can voice one's observations.

Next stop is Nethermost Pike, just ¼ mile and 15 minutes jog away. There's a descent down to the depression of Swallow Scarth, then a short climb onto the flat featureless stony desert of Nethermost Pike, although why it's called a 'Pike' I don't know because the word denotes a prominent peak and there is none to be seen. Then it's just half a mile and nine minutes, a similar descent and short climb up to Dollywaggon Pike, the southern terminus of the Helvellyn ridge. 'Dollywaggon' is a poetic name with prosaic origins, a dollywaggon being a sled-like barrow that was used for transporting stone down steep fellsides in the mining and quarrying industries of yesteryear – so there must have been some industrial activity in this vicinity at some point, perhaps down in Ruthwaite Cove. Anyway, the time is 17.05 and we need to keep moving.

Taking the Path Less Travelled

Trotting down the ridge from Dollywaggon summit I spy an old iron fence post to our right, which is a good marker. Some fifty yards to the left of the post is where we cross the path and make the direct drop to Grisedale Tarn. The tarn comes into view – a big one as tarns go, and this is quite a dramatic scene ahead, the massive bulk of Fairfield rearing up on the other side and the steep killer climb that lies ahead of us. The path zig-zags down to the tarn but we take a direct line down the grass and between the rocks, heading for the outflow beck on the eastern side. It's quite a steep and jarring descent, especially for legs which have been on the fells for eleven hours and which are aching now. Jim's legs are younger and fresher than mine and he bounds off ahead, enjoying going at his own pace. My legs may ache but it's okay, I'm in control and not going to go too hard down here. There's still some way to go before I can pull out all the stops.

We meet at the bottom of the steep slope and jog through the rocks and cross over the beck. There are some young wild campers pitched up nearby and walking around in the early evening sun. It's a classic wild camping spot and an idyllic place on a nice summer's early evening such as this. The water of the tarn is flat calm and it would be good to go swimming in there. We exchange greetings with a girl with long dark hair, and then I look out for the faint start of the path that we'll follow up and across this steep north-west face of Fairfield, in the direction of Cofa Pike. At the start of the path there's a good stream and I tell Jim that I need a drink and a bite to eat, that I'll take my time and he should carry on and I'll catch him – but that first I just need to get a Trek bar from the rucksack.

I'm thirsty and the cold stream water tastes good: pure mountain water unadulterated by chlorine or flouride or whatever else 'corporation pop' town water is tainted with. I fill my flat water bottle from where the stream spouts like a tap and gulp down a good amount. I then re-fill the bottle, rip off the Trek bar wrapper and take a bite. It's dense chewy stuff, this time chocolate-flavoured, and it needs helping down with some of the water. I need to just be stationary for a couple of minutes whilst I chew on the bar and drink some water and gather myself together for this big climb. The food and drink will pick me up, and this is a good point to be re-fuelling, with the climb far too steep for running. I eat the whole bar, and the energy that it will give me will be slowly released as we make the climb up Fairfield.

This path is not very well-used and isn't shown on the OS Explorer map. The usual way up Fairfield is from Grisedale Hause Gap, which is to the south of the tarn. That path is steep too, though not as steep as the one we're taking. I think that most BGR runners these days use the path via Hause Gap to Fairfield, which they then descend to go up Seat Sandal and down to Dunmail Raise. But the most direct and quickest way up Fairfield from the tarn is definitely the Cofa Pike one – and I know this because I've tried both and timed them. The Hause Gap path is a bit easier, but you only have to look on the map to see what a dog-leg it is, and it takes about ten minutes longer going up that way. The Cofa Pike path is also more adventurous and 'fun', I think.

I know that by most people's standards this is a strange idea of fun, but we are not most people, we are taking the path less travelled, and the fun is in the challenge of getting to grips (literally) with the mountain in a tougher and more intimate way than if we were to simply follow the more usual wide, eroded, part-paved and prodigiously-cairned 'tourist path'. And make no mistake, this fell is a mountain and we're on one of its more rugged mountainous aspects – the north-west face (the north-east face with its steep cliffs dropping into Deepdale being even more rugged). At 2,863' it's one of the highest in the Lake District, and this climb from Grisedale Tarn is over 1,000' and should take us 30 minutes.

From previous recces I know we have to be careful not to end up on the path that slants across the face to Deepdale Hause. Both routes start on the same path, but our path branches off steeply and directly up the face towards the pointed rocky subsidiary of Cofa Pike. When the body is tired it can have a mind of its own in following the line of least resistance, even if it's the *wrong* line. And there comes a point where the mind has to command the body to do things it doesn't really want to do anymore. It's part of the nature of the ultra-distance run. There is an element of forcing the body to do things above and beyond what is normally expected of it, and it can be painful and dispiriting. You can get to the stage where you ask yourself: 'Why am I doing this? What is the point?' The legs may ache, the pain of old injuries may return and the whole body may become weary. But perhaps the worst thing is that sense of futility about the whole project, which may descend and put the brakes on or even halt forward momentum. That hasn't happened to me here and now, though I have felt it on long runs in the past and I know it's commonly experienced on the Bob Graham and other ultra-distance rounds. I am struggling a bit to get going here, but I always knew this climb would be tough and I'm still mentally positive.

Over twenty years ago, when I was lodging with Keith Anderson in Ambleside, I went for a run up Fairfield, down to Grisedale Tarn, up Helvellyn, then all the way back to Ambleside via the tarn and Fairfield again. I told Keith where I'd been, and I remember him being impressed by what for me wasn't really a big deal at the time. I remember saying to him that 'You need a different set of muscles for those gradients' (up and down Dollywaggon Pike and

Fairfield via Grisedale Tarn), and he replied 'Yeah, muscles in the *mind*!' And yes, it's a mental sport is fell-running, or it's all in the mind – but *where* is the mind? Is it just inside the skull, or is it in the solar plexus, or maybe even the *legs*? Mind and body are intimately linked, of course, and cannot be entirely separated. The mind-body becomes inspired by the fell environment and the sense of freedom that comes from moving quickly and freely through it. Children run for the simple joy of it, without even thinking about it. And when we are young we can run naturally, without forcing it or struggling with it. When we get older we need to train for it, especially for fell-running, which is so demanding on the body. We set ourselves training schedules, racing goals, challenges, and we train our bodies to become fell-fit, and it's only really through the application of training and being fit that we can experience the joy of fell-running.

It's a joy which, once discovered, one wants to keep going. The 'buzz' of fell-running is difficult to replace. Injured fell-runners may walk the fells – which is still good, but doesn't give the same intensity of feeling. Many injured fell-runners take up cycling, which is something they might do anyway as part of their training when not injured. Some old fell-runners with chronic injuries who can't run anymore take up cycling full-time. An example is Billy Bland, who never cycled in his prime but is now (in his late sixties) very enthusiastic and accomplished on a bike. But unless injury prevents it, most fell-runners want to keep it going for as long as possible, and many manage to keep going after knee, hip and ankle operations. Personally, I suppose I've been lucky with regard to injuries, although I have had a lot of sprained ankles over the years. At one point my ankle was that bad that I thought I would have to give up the sport, but with time and patience it healed and I was back fell-running again. There are some who give up fell-running through injury or some other reason, but most want to keep it going – and *keeping it going* in a running life is the important thing, and especially as one gets older because when you get older and you stop it's harder to get going again.

Higher and Wilder

Keeping it going is what I intend to do, and what I am doing now as I ascend this steep face of Fairfield. Jim is now about fifty yards ahead of me, but that's fine, I'll catch him, or he'll have to wait for me. Lifting the legs up this loose rocky path is hard work, but my mind-body is engaging with the challenge and I'm making progress. It's a narrow path, not very well-used – which is not surprising, although it is shown in the hand-drawn map in the Wainwright guide. I think some BGR contenders do come this way, as I've seen stud marks up here before.

I stop to take a swig of water from the flat bottle I've kept in my hand, and I look down towards the tarn. Someone is in there swimming – the girl we saw with the long dark hair perhaps, and the early evening sunshine sparkles on the ripples she's created. Wild swimming is another way of engaging the mind-body with wild Nature. I've never swum in any of the high tarns, though I have, of course, swum in Rydal Water, and also Crummock Water. Crummock was a bit cold in just a pair of shorts, but Rydal Water, being quite shallow, can get relatively warm in the summer.

Swimming out into a lake you get a slightly different perspective on the fells, and it's another mode of self-propulsion, and of being in the natural environment – but I'd rather be fell-running.

Turning my attention to the task at hand I stow the water bottle back in the bum bag and get going. The gradient of the path eases off a little to take a more slanting angle, and Jim waits for me here. 'How are you feeling?' he asks. 'Fine, fine,' I say, and I go ahead and he follows close behind me. The gradient steepens again, so much so that we have to use our hands to haul ourselves up. Clutching at loose stones and sods of grass and moss, I say to Jim: 'I'm reduced to all fours – like an animal.' And there is something animal-like about fell-running, a throwback to basics, a de-civilising, a reverting to some fundamental sense of being human that feels positive and good. Perhaps this reduction of life to being a struggle in a wild natural environment resonates in our race memory DNA to a time when we were Palaeolithic hunter-gatherers – long before the days of smart phones, supermarkets, mortgages, schools, governments, televisions, motor cars and various other modern inventions which in some ways seem to have made us less, rather than more human.

On all fours, clutching at red-tinted stones of scree and grabbing at lumps of soft moss, my eyes are not far from the ground and see the wonders of Nature in her small details. The piece of ground I hold in my right hand is a complex universe of grass and moss combined, and on some of these stones grow grey-green lichens that look like miniature trees. Here there is a little scattering of hard brown sheep droppings – and it's amazing how sheep will get just about anywhere on the fells. A little higher and there are some delicate little vivid green ferns and some pretty yellow flowers that have escaped the nibblings of the rapacious Herdwick. Up we go, higher and wilder into the fellcosm, the grass and moss giving way to dry scree slopes, shifting beneath hands and feet so that there is some sliding down as well as climbing up. Finally the gradient eases off and we find ourselves just below and to the side of the distinctive configuration of rocks at the top of Cofa Pike. Something about the shape of this gnarly knobble is interesting and suggestive of it being imbued with some kind of significance beyond just being a random jumble of rocks, but I guess it's 'just' a characterful fell feature. Here there is a cairn, and the path turns right to take a circuitous route to the Fairfield summit plateau, but the quickest way is the most direct way and so I'll lead Jim up the steep scramble through the rocks ahead of us.

One winter I came up here from the tarn through slippery slushy snow. Wearing running gear and without an ice axe I had to be very careful on some of the snow slopes, kicking steps with my flimsy fell shoes and digging in my gloved fingers to get a purchase. I was worried about slipping and sliding a long way down into the rocks. The adrenaline was pumping and my heart beating fast as I had to contend with the danger, as well as the physical effort. Although the snow was mostly soft, the slope was very steep, and there could've been icy patches beneath the snow. I felt a bit of a fool for not having even considered that it would be like this, and for not having brought an ice axe (not that I had one), but there was nothing to do but to plough on as to have gone back would've been even worse. When I got to this level shelf near Cofa Pike I breathed a sigh of relief, but the worst was yet to come. This final steep slope ahead, before the summit plateau, was a massive bank of steep snow, which definitely had hard frozen patches in it. I tried three different routes, one directly ahead, one to the left a bit by the rocks, and the other where the circuitous path was buried. But at each attempt I bottled out and back-tracked, wary of getting into a slide and not being able to stop myself. I was almost in despair. I didn't want to turn back the same way I'd come, which could've been equally dangerous. And then, as luck would have it, three guys appeared at the top of the snow bank. 'How did you get down there?' one of them shouted to me. 'I've come up from Grisedale Tarn,' I said. They were wanting to come down to head for St. Sunday Crag, via Cofa Pike. They had ice axes and crampons so I encouraged them down, then I borrowed an ice axe to get myself safely up the snow bank and then threw it down the slope to them. I was so relieved and thankful for their help. Now that I was on the summit plateau I knew I'd be all right.

That story may serve as a cautionary tale about the dangers of fell-running or walking in winter conditions. Conditions may seem fine for running on lower slopes or shallow slopes, but on the high fells and on steep slopes you can get into difficulty quite suddenly. It's a good idea to carry an ice axe on the back of your rucksack, in case you need it. Crampons are obviously no use on fell-running shoes, but you can get strap-on spikes, which I'm sure are very useful in certain conditions, although I've never used them myself. But an ice axe is much more useful as a safety aid when traversing steep snowy/icy slopes, mainly as a brake to stop yourself sliding if you slip, but also as a probe and anchor point on your way up.

A short scramble up the rocks brings us to the summit plateau of Fairfield. We jog to the cairn at the highest point and I note the time on the schedule card: 17.47 (just 27 minutes from Grisedale Tarn). I've been up here so many times over the years, usually as part of the 'horseshoe' from Rydal or Ambleside. I've been up on my own, on club runs and in both the Fairfield Horseshoe and the Rydal Round races. I prefer the Rydal Round because there's only one checkpoint – at the top of Fairfield, which allows for off-the-path contouring routes around the summits of Great Rigg, Hart Crag and Dove Crag – and so requires some judgement, or 'fell-craft'. Also the Rydal Round is part of the Ambleside Sports – a big Lakeland fair incorporating the traditional Lakeland sport of Cumberland and Westmorland wrestling, and also grass track cycle racing, track running, races for children and a short 'guides'-style fell race. There are also lots of food and craft stalls, a beer tent, a brass band and an entertaining commentary over a loud speaker. All in all it's a great social event that attracts locals and visitors alike.

Looking southwards from the summit we can just see the lake of Windermere shining in the distance, and to the left the top of the Wansfell ridge. Ambleside is just out of view but we know it's not far away from here – 5¼ miles to the Golden Rule in fact, according to my measurements. We are on the 'home straight' now. It's not all downhill, but mostly downhill, with only about 550' left of climbing. We set off jogging across the summit rocks, bearing left to pick up the curving path around the top of a scree gully, and then picking up speed over the grass to the left of the path, contouring round a rocky knobble on the racing line, a fellrunners' trod that follows a clever way on grass, avoiding the worst of the rocky path down to the col and then joining the path on the short easy climb up to Hart Crag.

Feels Like I'm Flying

At the Hart Crag summit cairn the time is 17.58, which means we should be in Ambleside in less than an hour. We veer right off the path to pick up the grassy running trod that picks its way through the rocks down to the col and the broken-down stone wall. We cross over to the left of the wall here, follow the stony path a short way and then veer off left to take a more direct and grassy line towards Dove Crag. I'm feeling strong and setting the pace, which is beginning to feel like race pace as we climb steadily up the grassy ridge.

It takes us 12 minutes to get to the summit, which is a rock platform topped by a cairn, some twenty yards to the left of the wall. I remember being a checkpoint marshal here in the Fairfield Horseshoe Race some years ago. The runners had a tendency to just follow the line of the wall and I had to shout over to a lot of them to come to the summit so that I could note their number on the clipboard. It can be hard getting everyone's number when a lot of people go through in a group. Some runners make it easy for the marshal by running up close and showing their number, or shouting it out, but others can be deep in their own 'zone' and not very helpful. It's important to get everyone's number, or at least the total number of runners visiting the checkpoint.

Helping out as a marshal, or in some other capacity, at a fell race is a good thing to do as it's a 'giving back' to the community of the sport, which can be taken for granted. Many fell races are organised on a not-for-profit basis, or just a minimal profit for the organiser, and sometimes they may even make a loss. Entry fees are usually kept small – enough to cover a modest prize list, perhaps the renting of a field for car-parking, and perhaps some post-race tea and cake. Some popular races are organised by running clubs and are money makers for the coffers, but that's okay as the money generally goes towards such as paying rent for a clubhouse or subsidising championship race trips etc.

Marshals are volunteers who give up their time for free and sometimes have to stand for hours in exposed conditions and bad weather on the fell tops, and without them the races couldn't be run. But the marshal can get something out of the experience, as well as putting in. For the runner who would normally be in the race but who has opted to marshal due to injury, lack of fitness or whatever it can give a different perspective on the sport. It's interesting to see how the front runners usually make it look very easy, looking comfortable in themselves, moving fluidly and apparently effortlessly, and often way ahead of the majority. Further down the field you see some people struggling and looking quite *un*-comfortable – staggering and wheezing and with pained expressions, such that the average non-fell-runner could be forgiven for asking the question 'Why?'. It looks masochistic, and perhaps it is for some people, but pushing the body to its limits at whatever ability brings its own satisfactions, if only the relief at the end when it's all over. There's no getting away from the fact that to really enjoy fell-racing you have to get yourself race-fit, which takes a lot of hard work. Some runners do have a lot of natural ability, but everyone has to train if they want to do well – and 'doing well' is not just a question of achieving a certain level of performance in terms of time or position, but ultimately means enjoying the experience.

We're not in an actual race today but we are now 'racing' down from Dove Crag, crossing over the wall and really opening up on the fast grassy section that leads to the next top of High Pike. And my ability to do this, after already being on the hoof for 45 miles and 12 hours is down to the months of training I've done leading up to it, as well as my many years' experience of fell-running. I love this section, and it feels like I'm really flying now, totally focussed, co-ordinated, in control and in the moment. There is no question of 'Why?' because I am loving this right now and it's just what I do, a sort of self-expression, a communion with the living Earth, a celebratory dance over the fell-body.

Down, down we go, over the summit-lump of High Pike, which is just a gentle rise on the grassy ridge. The summit cairn is on the other side of the wall but the highest point is on this side. I quickly slide my bum bag round to note the time – 18.20, before charging down towards Low Pike. We pick our way through rocks and scamper down steep slopes, follow fiddly trods, at one point running over a massive flat rock. It's constantly changing, a dance downwards through an obstacle course of rocks and grass, the wall constantly on our left hand side. Some years ago I saw a grey squirrel running along the top of this wall, a bit higher up towards High Pike. It was a strange sight as you don't expect to see squirrels up here, out of their usual woodland habitat. I guess this one was a bit of an adventurer, just up here for the hell of it, as I doubt there'd be any food for it on the fell. And I suppose I am an adventurer too, out of my usual woodland habitat, although the fells are also a sort of habitat for me.

Now we're climbing up to Low Pike, the highest point of which is the wall that runs over the crest of the ridge. This used to be a second checkpoint in the Rydal Round race, and from here it was a descent to the right through head-high bracken on a path down to the cheering crowds at Ambleside Sports. The wall is broken down at this point so it's easy to cross over to the other side. The time is 18.29. I look out for Rob Sparkes, who's supposed to be meeting us here to take some photos, but I can't see him. I shout out his name but there's no reply. Ambleside is now plainly in view, its grey stone and white-painted buildings catching the western sun, and the tall elegant spire of St. Mary's Church a beacon for this fell-wanderer's homecoming – back to where I once belonged, and back to the start of the round. It's a beautiful setting for a settlement, nestled between Loughrigg to the west and Wansfell to the east, the Fairfield Horseshoe to the north, and Lake Windermere to the south.

Ambleside is like a smaller version of Keswick really, though with a different, a softer feel about it. I've lived on both sides of the Raise and have felt at home in both, but perhaps feel a bit more at home in South Lakes, which is where I've mostly found stronger social connections. It's partly because of my involvement with Ambleside AC over the years, and also the greater period of time spent living and working on the south side. But also it might be because I grew up in Lancashire and so feel more akin to South Lakes people, many of whom also grew up in Lancashire. Before the county of Cumbria was introduced in 1974 much of South Lakes fell within the northern part (the Furness part) of Lancashire, the border stretching as far as Brathay, just outside of Ambleside, although Ambleside itself fell within the county of Westmorland. I've been drawn north of the Raise for the fells, which are bigger and wilder and more spacious, and also for jobs, but when push comes to shove I have to admit that I am more a man of the South Lakes. I've migrated between the two over the years, but there comes a point where one has to plump for one or the other.

It's a steep scramble down grass from the wall to the main path, and then further down again to another path that skirts round to the east of the wall. As we approach a boggy area ahead I see a lone figure with long dark hair and realise that it's Rob, with his camera – now aiming the camera at us to get some shots. I shout out a greeting, he waves, then as we get closer and he gets another shot I shout to him that we're going to veer left away from him and round the bog. It's okay because he's got some photos now and I shout again 'See you in the Rule!'

We pass a small green sign on a wooden stake that says 'DEEP BOG' and 'PATH', with an arrow pointing away from the bog towards the wall, but I go in the opposite direction, having come this way numerous times before and knowing that it's possible to skirt round the worst of the bog, which is quicker than following the path by the wall that is an awkward mixture of mud and rocks. Some years ago a walker sank in the bog – up to his chest I think, and had to be rescued by the local mountain rescue team. That's an unusual occurrence on the fells, but a strong warning not to try and go straight across this boggy area, which must be worse than it looks.

The dance continues through grass and rock, as I pick the optimum line – which I know from my many recces. A couple of minutes after the bog there's a sharp left hand turn onto a path that runs alongside some crags and avoids the difficult rock step on the main path. It curves to the right and becomes a hard stony path, uncomfortable on the feet in my flimsy fell shoes after the soft grass. There are plenty of rocky trip hazards and I need to really concentrate here. I may be moving well but my legs are tired, which increases the risk of catching a toe on a rock and falling headlong. So 'Concentrate and keep it going' I tell myself in my head.

I guess most fell-runners talk to themselves in their heads, inspiring themselves to keep going, to run faster, harder, stronger. In races the mind can try to thrash the body into doing what it wants – shouting and swearing and even insulting the self in order to push the body into the best possible result. Some runners even verbalise this out loud. I remember racing with the Keswick AC runner Mark Denham-Smith some years ago and he was angrily shouting and swearing behind me. I thought he was shouting at me at first, but he later explained that he was shouting at himself!

The stony path terminates at a wall and a stony track, and here we take a direct line over the soft grass, cutting the corner to pick up the track lower down at a gate. Through the gate and then after a hundred yards I suddenly drop down the steep bank on the left to Low Sweden Bridge. From the bridge we go through the yard at Nook End Farm, and now we're on the tarmacked surface of Nook Lane. This is definitely the 'home straight' now, with only about half a mile to go. The lane is downhill, and I pick up speed down here, going as fast as I can and leaving Jim behind. Past the dog kennels up on the left and the B&Bs on the right, then the ginnel into the Greenbank estate on the right (where I'm reminded of the punishing hill interval sessions we used to do there on dark winter Thursday evenings, Keith shouting encouragement to us as we went round and round, up and down, training for a fell season and a British Champs campaign). How many miles of running and feet of climbing have I done in my life to arrive at this point, which is surely a milestone in my fell-running 'career'? All that matters now is the here and now of sprinting along this stretch of tarmac, now climbing slightly to the junction of the Kirkstone Road, where Ben suddenly appears from around a corner and takes a photo of me with his phone. It's all smiles as I jog the short distance up Kirkstone road to the front door of The Golden Rule pub, where I check my watch, dig out the schedule card and note the final time: 18.51, 12 minutes from Low Pike and 12 hours, 36 minutes for the whole round. Jim and Ben jog up to join me, Christeen appears and she takes a photo of the three of us outside the front of the pub, below the colourful flowers of a hanging basket. And that's it – round completed, job done, and I'm happy just to have completed it, but even happier to have got round in a good time (44 minutes faster than scheduled), without distress and feeling good. All the planning and training has come to fruition, and it's an achievement I am pleased with.

Jim gets his bag from Ben and we walk up to my car by the old church to get changed. In the car the Stooges tape rests halfway out of the hi-fi cassette slot: music to fell-dance to, music for self-rewilding. But now it's time for relaxing and unwinding, socialising, beer-drinking and de-briefing. Today's adventure in the 'wilderness' is over and now it's time to return to civilisation and social life. Changed, we saunter down the road to join Ben and Christeen at The Golden Rule.

The Golden Rule

Beer-drinking and fell-running have gone together in my mind for as long as I can remember, and certainly ever since I joined Ambleside Athletic Club, whose training runs are traditionally followed by a visit to the pub. On summer evenings and Sunday mornings the pub could be anywhere in South Lakes, depending on where the scheduled training run is taking place. Favourites in the past have included: The Travellers Rest, Grasmere; The Brittania, Elterwater; The Sun, Coniston; The Tower Bank Arms, Near Sawrey; The Drunken Duck, Barngates; The Badger Bar, Rydal; The Brookside, Windermere; The Watermill, Ings; The Blacksmiths, Broughton Mills; The Three Shires, Little Langdale; The Old Dungeon Ghyll, Langdale; The Mortal Man or The Queens, Troutbeck. But the 'basecamp' pub for winter Tuesday evenings is The Golden Rule in Ambleside. And what better place for a fell-runners' meet?

Ever since I've known it the Rule has been a pub favoured by outdoorsy folk as a place to refresh after a walk, climb, run, bike or whatever they've been up to in the outdoor playground. It's always had a good mixture of locals, students and visitors and is renowned for its convivial atmosphere – which is helped by the fact that no meals are served, there is no 'piped' music and no television (except sometimes in the secluded back room). There's a good range of well-kept Robinsons ales, and genuinely friendly service from the bar staff. It's a place where you can go on your own to read the paper or chat to whoever happens to be there, or it's a place where you can meet up with friends. When I was doing my round recces I would often come here afterwards to write up my notes in my notebook and it's the sort of place where you can feel comfortable doing that. In the summer it's nice to sit out the back, which is a nice little sun-trap in the late afternoon.

Some people who take their athletic endeavours very seriously shun beer, or other alcoholic drinks. And, to be fair, some people – and especially younger people these days – just don't like drinking much at all. But most of the best fell-athletes have been, and still are, beer-drinkers, and in moderation it seems to complement the activity. When you are doing plenty of training you soon burn off the calories, it's a refreshing reward after a hard workout or race, and it's full of beneficial nutrients: protein, carbohydrates, B vitamins and a host of useful minerals. The health benefits of moderate beer drinking are many. Dark ales and stouts are generally the healthiest, as they are highest in antioxidants, and 'living' ale from the cask is much better than pasteurized in bottles or cans. Beer is also mostly water, which makes it a good hydrating drink. It 'puts the sweat back in', as William Cobbett said. Of course it can be *de*-hydrating if you have too much, but all in all, *in moderation* it not only does you no harm but is positively good for the health.

Beer-drinking can also be good for fell race performances. I recall an interview with top fell-runner Jack Maitland in *The Fellrunner* magazine in the mid-eighties in which he said that one secret of his success was to drink a good few pints of real ale the evening before the race. And Keith Anderson had a storming run at the Sedbergh Hills Race the day after he'd had a skinful at a clubmate's wedding reception. I'm not sure, but I think this may have been in 1991, the year he broke the course record (which still stands today). Also Joss Naylor in an interview once advised the novice fell-runner to 'Get plenty of Guinness and cider down thee' (as well as plenty of fell miles in the legs, of course). It doesn't work for everyone, and I don't want to encourage irresponsible drinking. Moderation is, of course, the key – although 'moderation' is at different levels for different people, and for many it probably doesn't match the government guidelines. Anyway, beer-drinking in moderation is positively healthy.

At the bar Ben buys us pints of Dizzy Blonde, a 'zesty blonde ale' that is crisp, clean and refreshing, and which is the perfect tipple for a summer's evening after a long day on the fell. 'Cheers!' we say, and the four of us take a table in the corner by the window. I don't feel like I've run as far as I have, just pleasantly physically tired, happy with the achievement and happy to be with friends. I gulp down a goodly amount of ale and it hits the spot very nicely indeed. Rob comes through the door, gets himself a pint and sits down to join us. 'Cheers!' again, and 'Well done!' 'I've got some good shots,' he says. 'You were flying.' And we talk about the whole thing, how it went, the first solitary section, the meeting with Ben and Christeen at Honister, the 'flying' along the High Spy – Cat Bells ridge, the bad patch going up Latrigg, the meeting up with Jim, the slight difficulties with the timekeeping, and the triumphal sprint home. It's good to talk about it and get the input from those who helped me to make it happen and to whom I am grateful. And without this celebratory, beery de-briefing the ending would've felt like an empty anti-climax. To have friends who have believed in it and supported it makes it all the more worthwhile.

We go into the fell 'wilderness', often alone, to re-wild and re-vitalise ourselves, but there is always a return to human society and to friends. The long solitary fell run can be a powerful and positive thing in one's inner life, but human life is only fully human when it includes the social life. And what better place to socialise than a public house? The pub's very purpose is to facilitate the social.

Another pint! It's my round in more ways than one and I go up to the bar to get us all another drink. Behind the bar, suspended from the ceiling, is a large ornamental brass rule with calibrated lines – in reference clearly to the pub's name. There are two theories as to the origin of the name. The first is that it comes from the Bible, Book of Matthew, Chapter 7, Verse 12, and Jesus' Sermon on the Mount: 'Therefore all things whatever ye would that men should do to you, do you even to them'. Put more simply as 'Do unto others as you would have them do unto you', this ethic of reciprocity is known as 'the golden rule'. I have seen a picture of an old postcard of the sign that once hung outside the pub and which refers to this meaning. It depicts two female figures in long dresses looking at each other, one with her arms outstretched as if in appeal to the other, and illuminated by a sort of spotlight within a flower from above – the light of God presumably, and the words 'Do to others as you would be done by' at the bottom. It was possibly painted by one of the students of the Royal College of Art, who were evacuated to Ambleside between 1940-1945, and who frequented the pub.

The other theory as to the origin of the name is that at one time 'the golden rule' meant that a pub possessed only a beer licence and was prohibited from selling wines and spirits, and also from opening on Sundays. This was intended to ensure that agricultural and other local workers abstained from alcohol on the Lord's Day, when church attendance was expected. Some 150 years ago many pubs had the name 'The Golden Rule' in reference to this particular kind of licence, but as much of the rural population moved to industrial towns, where pubs were open seven days a week, the opening hours gradually changed in rural areas and pubs became allowed to open on Sundays. Pubs that had been called 'The Golden Rule' changed their names when the old rule no longer applied and they were allowed to sell all drinks, including on Sundays. However, The Golden Rule in Ambleside kept its name and is now only one of two pubs in Britain with the name, the other one being in Edinburgh.

Our Golden Rule became an inn around the mid-eighteenth century, and was a brew-house of the old Ambleside Hall estate before then. Situated in the oldest part of Ambleside on Smithy Brow, leading to the Kirkstone Road, it was on the main road north before the Rydal Road became the main road in 1833. There have been many licensees over the years, and customers have been a rich mixture of locals and visitors. The inn was occasionally used as a courthouse during the 19th century and parties sometimes took place in the 'ballroom'. There were households in the main building and also in the outbuildings of the yard, where there were also stables, a hayloft, general stores and a joinery. ST Coleridge's son Hartley sometimes drank here, as well as Thomas De Quincey (and possibly STC himself, though probably not Wordsworth). In 1921 the Rule was sold to Hartleys Brewery (no relation to Coleridge jnr). In 1969 Alfred Wainwright, the guide book writer, visited and had a meal here. In the 1980s the Rule became a mecca for British climbers, including Bill Birkett, Chris Bonnington, Tony Greenbank, Doug Scott, Pete Whillance and Don Whillans, who all regularly met here with the landlord John Lockley. In the '90s it became a centre for paragliders, John being a keen paraglider himself. And now it is again the pub where Ambleside AC come after winter evening training runs.

At one time advertised as 'Just an Old-fashioned Country Inn', the Rule used to offer accommodation until the mid '70s and meals until around 1990, but these days offers neither and is essentially just a drinking establishment. Food consists of the usual bar snacks of crisps and nuts, and also pork pies and scotch eggs – which are made by the butcher Freddie Garside just around the corner on North Road. John Lockley has been the landlord since 1981, and is now ably assisted by manager John Wrennall. It may be 'just' a drinking establishment, but this essence of what a pub is all about is largely what makes it special.

The pub is a symbol of freedom, a place to go to get away from work and home-life – somewhere to send away the trials of life with beer and conversation. It's a place where you can discuss ideas, plans and 'put the world to rights'. From the mid to late eighteenth century visiting the pub was sometimes a political act, as it became a form of protest against the emerging new work 'ethic' of the Industrial Revolution, and also the Temperance Movement of the Methodist Church. Ale itself became a symbol of freedom – freedom from the church, gentry, and factory. Pubs became the focus for meetings of dissatisfied workers and radical elements who saw themselves becoming enslaved to their capitalist masters. But community pub culture became progressively eroded as tax was introduced on beer sales and 'free' alehouses were taken over by the big breweries to become tied houses. Informal 'home-brew' pubs became criminalized and especially rural pubs were closing down in large numbers from as early as the mid-19th century. Thankfully, there are plenty left in the Lake District.

Pubs and beer-drinking have long played a central role in binding communities together. These days, of course, there's been a decline in real communities and more and more people are inclined to stay at home and drink at home out of a bottle or a can, often in front of a television or computer screen. Going to the public house to drink real ale and have real face-to-face conversations with other people is a positive political act – an active protest against the prevailing culture of staying in and staring at a screen (or even going out just to stare at a screen).

Right now I'm staring at a row of hand pumps for a selection of Robinsons ales. I'm told that four of these hand pumps have been in service ever since 1932. The pump clip on the Dizzy Blonde depicts a sexy-looking young blonde woman in a sitting position, wearing a skimpy red dress, red shoes and red lipstick, showing a lot of leg and staring seductively at me. It's a blatantly sexist image that harks back to a less politically-correct era when it was commonplace to sell products on sexual images. It's perhaps a bit like those Big D 'babe boards' carrying rows of salted peanuts you used to get in pubs in the '70s and '80s, and each pack of nuts sold would reveal more of a sexy scantily-clad woman underneath. Looking at the Dizzy Blonde picture now I think it's amusing, and I guess it's supposed to be 'ironic' in a retro sexist way. I can't imagine anyone finding it offensive, but you never know. Dizzy Blonde is a 'zesty ale with wild, aromatic, invigorating Amarillo hops', which is a pretty sexy description.

Anyway, I get the drinks in and take them back to our table – and we won't be having any more than this as some of us have some driving to do. Ben and Christeen will be going back to their home in Keswick, Rob to Grasmere, and myself to the wood. Jim lives in Ambleside with his wife Karen, so he doesn't have to worry, but the two of us will be going for fish and chips at The Old Smithy and we'll have to go soon if we're going to make it in time before last orders for the sit-down area. We've got twenty minutes though yet – time to enjoy more beer and the bonhomie of our little group. Ben talks about his own big days out in the fells of walking a whole book of Wainwrights in a day, Jim talks of how he'd like to do the BGR, but that he might have a go at my SFR before that. Rob is not ideally built for running. He has done some and enjoyed it, but found he kept getting injured so he prefers to stick to walking and climbing. Christeen too is not a runner, but a strong walker and fell-lover, who actually grew up on a fell farm, 'Fell End Farm' – truly a fellender.

The time has come to drain our glasses and go our different ways – and it's always good to go our *own* way, especially if it's a bit different to the well-trodden, the conventional. The culture of fell-running celebrates individuals who wilfully go their own way and yet who are still a part of the fell fraternity by virtue of that common quest for, and enjoyment of, outer and inner wildness. 'A wilderness is rich with liberty', as Wordsworth said. Or Jay Griffiths in her excellent book *Wild: An Elemental Journey*: 'To be most alive is to be most free is to be most wild.' For me, fell-running is about wildness, freedom and feeling alive – and to be the most alive one can be is surely not a bad objective and way of life.

The Real Work

Waking to the sound of raindrops drumming on the skin of the flysheet – the inside of the tent turned into the sound box of a percussive instrument. In the background the sound of rushing water in the beck, more voluminous in sound and quantity than usual. There must've been a lot of rain during the latter part of the night. I put on my reading glasses and they instantly steam up. I was going to try writing my journal in the tent but the humidity in here is going to keep steaming up the specs so it's not worth it. I get dressed in the cramped damp confines and exit my polyester front door to greet another day. I go for a pee by the base of the fallen beech tree and then put the kettle on and get my breakfast stuff together – banana, muesli, coffee. I feel relaxed from a good night's sleep. My legs ache from yesterday's epic run, but mentally I'm still on a high.

When I got back to camp last night I lit a fire and sat in the chair, just staring at the flames, drinking a couple of cans of lager, still buzzing from my big day out. I got up in the middle of the night for a pee and it was raining a bit then, but it must've come on heavy after that. It would be good to see an updated forecast, but of course I have no access to the internet here. I'm completely off-grid and without a reliable mobile phone signal. Not far from civilisation, but cut off from it. No electricity, no TV, no computer, no house-mates – just trees and birds for company. The rain eases off whilst I have my breakfast, but now, as I sit in the chair beneath the tarp it comes on heavy again. I could sit here and wait for it to stop before I get out and about, but it might rain like this all day for all I know. I listen to the sound of it pattering on the tarp, and also to the constant coo-cooing of a wood pigeon. The big log from last night's fire is still gently smoking and fragrancing the air, despite having been rained on for hours – smouldering on, against the odds. Anyway, I'm going to have to make a move and drive into Ambleside to go to work in the shop.

It's a wet Saturday morning and the outdoor shops are going to be busy with folk looking for waterproof jackets and over-trousers, or just browsing around and sheltering from the rain. I clock on at 10am and Sharon goes through the daily targets with me. The muzak is on and some auto-tuned warbler is singing 'everything's going to be all right, everything's going to be okay', which of course it isn't. Things are far from being all right here as far as I'm concerned. I started the day still on my running high, but now I feel my spirits quickly slump, faced with a day in this place. And yet I feel a core mental strength, and a determination not to be conquered by the situation. I feel contempt for this shop, though not for the masses who cross the threshold in search of a cheap waterproof or just some shelter from the weather. Our 'conversion' figure is going to be very low today – which is to say the sensor at the door will register a high footfall, but only a small percentage of those who enter will actually buy anything.

And so the floorspace soon fills up with dripping wet customers, or rather *potential* customers, who mill around, idly browsing through the rails, some avoiding eye contact, others making some cheery clichéd comment like 'Nice weather for ducks!' or 'If there was no rain there'd be no lakes!' A family with young kids comes in with the definite objective of getting the kids kitted out with over-trousers. I show the mother to the stand with the lightweight ones and we search through for the right sizes by age category. We manage to find what she wants – a pair each for the kids, and so that's a bit of positive action and some job satisfaction, so maybe it's not so bad after all. But the general feeling I have is of being crushed, imprisoned in a place I don't want to be, and I don't know for how long I can stand it here before I hand in my notice and leave. But I suppose I can't just leave with nothing else to go to.

My *curriculum vitae*, modified though it was when I applied for this job, would not look good to most employers. I guess there is only so much modification (leaving stuff out basically) that can be done. As a fifty-year-old it wouldn't be appropriate to describe my whole work-life history, which could fill a book, but there can be no denying that I've moved around in jobs a lot and the longest time I've stayed in a job is just two-and-a-half years. I've had a hell of a lot of jobs by most people's standards – but so what? What, if anything, does it *mean*? That I am a restless personality that hates to feel tied down in a job and so is forever moving on? What is the root of this restlessness? It's a dissatisfaction with what is offered by the world of jobs, coupled with dissatisfaction with what accommodation is available (and I've also had a lot of addresses). I suppose we live in a world where to 'get on in the world' requires settling down and committing oneself to an employer, to having a 'career', to suppressing natural wild nomadic instincts and succumbing to a tamed routine, a lifetime of wage-slavery, domestication, boredom and quiet desperation. To be sure, the settled life of the committed employee, coupled with the settled domestic married and mortgaged life has its benefits. It is condoned and rewarded by the State, the system, and it is basically safe to live by the rules of that system. One feels a sense of security within the sheepfold of conformity, and one can feel oneself to be on the moral high ground when passing judgement on those who do not wish to or who are unable to join the fold.

What is *life*? In this society it is very much wrapped up in what you do, as in what you do for a living, your work, your job, your career. Plus of course your hobbies, if you've got any, and your partner and family, if you've got one. It is assumed by the government that this country is composed of families. Everyone is expected to have a family or to be part of a family, preferably a '*hard-working* family'. The nuclear family is a safe social unit – tamed, domesticated, imprisoned by financial commitment and responsibilities. The nest is feathered, and it goes without saying that life is all about making money and spending money – and in bringing up one's offspring to do likewise. And yet there is still a basic human instinct and need for wildness and freedom, which is largely suppressed.

As for me, where did my course of life, my *curriculum vitae*, start? I was born to parents, given a name and grew up in a house with a sister. I was required to go to school, where I enjoyed learning and making friends. As I got older and became more independent-minded I came to realise that most of what was being taught in school was a lot of information that would have nothing to do with my own life. Also I could see that it was all a form of social control, a sort of prison and a training ground for conformity in 'the real world'. But I carried on studying and achieving high grades because it provided the promise of leaving home to go away to university – and I desperately wanted to leave home because I wasn't happy living there. So after my 'A' levels I left school to study for a degree at college, where again I was increasingly struck by the irrelevance of most of it. I lost my appetite for studying and I got drunk on my new-found freedom away from family life. I dropped out, and then embarked on a long string of jobs and periods of unemployment. I worked as a labourer, barman, insurance clerk, shop assistant, civil servant, youth hostel warden, cook, gardener, estate worker, kitchen porter, showroom manager, campsite warden, chef, cleaner, painter, boat driver, bookseller, warehouse assistant, etcetera, etcetera. On my life-journey so far the job at the outdoor shop will be about my hundredth, and also the camp at the wood will be about my hundredth address (if you could call it a proper address). I suppose it would be fair to say that I've been a bit of a wanderer, footloose, though not exactly carefree. My address wanderings have mostly been motivated by a search to find somewhere affordable and *peaceful* where I can relax and think and be creative. And as for jobs, I have had some good ones, but they've mostly been situations of minimum wage-slavery that haven't provided the wherewithal to find a long-term satisfactory place to live and which have provided little in the way of job satisfaction (although some have provided friends, and also writing material). The 'real work' for me, for the last twenty years or so, has been *writing*, although I've earned precious little from it, and the necessity of going out to work in jobs that I don't really want to do has sapped my spirit and frustrated my creative output.

What is 'work'? I think a distinction can be made between just a job, which is undertaken primarily or solely to fulfil economic commitments – in particular paying the rent or mortgage, and the vocation or métier – where one works at something one has a gift for in order to serve the fellow human community. The idea of service has been muddied when so many jobs are in large companies where the only people that are really being served are the remote owners or shareholders, and yet still it is a basic human instinct or need to do some sort of useful work for the benefit of others. And so much the better if that work is carried out in some sociable environment as part of a team. The ideal sort of occupation combines work and pleasure into a coherent whole so that the expression 'work/life balance' becomes meaningless.

Writing is a lonely occupation, and not only do I need to work in a job for money, but I also need a sociable job to balance the long hours spent on my own. Most jobs in the Lake District fit this bill, being in the 'service sector', which revolves mainly around hospitality, catering and retail. I've worked in youth hostels, cafés, pubs, outdoor shops and food shops and they've all been temporary or disposable jobs, rather than career jobs. Many people like me who move to the Lake District have given up on their former jobs in some town or city, having seen through the myth of the modern-day career and having developed a life-view that prioritizes living over toiling in the work/life balance. Time becomes more important than money.

I've had some periods of unemployment and these have provided the opportunity to get stuck into writing, and enabled me to work on a number of novels and to get three of them published (*Black Sail, The Purple House* and *Down West)*. I was on the dole for a few months before I got the job at the shop – and, although I didn't do a lot of writing during that period, those months were useful in enabling the planning and training for yesterday's round of the fells. However, living on benefits gets ever harder and one finds oneself getting into debt and being asked to leave one's digs, and so getting a job becomes necessary to survive. There is a relative abundance of jobs in the Lake District, although getting one isn't as easy as it used to be, and finding affordable accommodation gets harder than ever.

The 'real work' of writing might be perceived by some people as being an escape from the real world of working in a job, of being 'hard-working' and materialistically aspirational and basically playing the game that the government wants us to play, keeping the head down and thinking about money, keeping busy and not asking too many questions and basically being an obedient materialistic tax-paying, non-complaining citizen in the consumer society. And as for creativity – who's got time for that? But if you are creative in some way you may feel that the expression of your creativity is a necessity and perhaps the only thing that makes life worth living. Far from being an escape from life, creative activity *adds* life – as does running, which is a form of self-expression and in a way creative. Fell-running is in some ways an escape – a running to the hills, a bid for freedom, albeit a temporary freedom from the world of money and jobs and 'the madding crowd'. But it is also an escape *to*, a freedom *for* something positive: a communion with Nature and a rewilding of consciousness that enriches our life and ultimately makes us more human.

A Room to Write

At lunchtime I get out to the Picnic Box for my usual cheese ploughman's roll, and I have to wait in a small queue of people – some tourists, and also some people from other outdoor shops. It's pouring down with rain and the streets of Ambleside are thronging. This is the heart of the madding crowd and the giant cash register. At the Market Cross war memorial there should be an electronic scoreboard displaying the running sales totals of all the outdoor shops.

Back in the shop I eat my cheese ploughman's roll at a desk in a very untidy stock room. There are rails and boxes of clothes and footwear everywhere. The company warehouse sends us two big deliveries every week and there's more stuff that comes in than goes out as sales, so the place is rammed to the gunnels with stock and it's impossible to know where everything is. Sharon is not allowed to send anything back. Instead we are simply expected to sell more to make more space. Sometimes the manager of the Bowness branch will take some stock off our hands, but the general picture is of more and more stuff coming in rather than going out. To be fair, Sharon could make more of an effort to put the stockrooms into a tidier and more orderly state. Quite often it's embarrassing when serving a customer with footwear and they need a particular size and the computer says we have a pair in stock but it's impossible to find them because the boxes are all over the place with different styles mixed together and the same style in two completely different places. The stockroom is in chaos basically, and trying to find what you want for a customer is frequently a fruitless search and a lost sale.

Clocking back on for the afternoon there's a lot of rail-tidying to do and the place 'looks like a bombsite' with garments all over the place, quite a lot fallen off hangers onto the floor, which is quite wet near the front door. There aren't so many people in the shop just now so there's room to manoeuvre as Paul and I take one half each of the shop and systematically work our way through the rails, putting things in the right place, in size order, with all the face-on garments presented as neatly as possible. This takes us the best part of an hour, by which time the rain has stopped and I volunteer to take a load of cardboard down to the recycling bins – which is a good opportunity to get out of the shop for some fresh air.

By and by my working day is over. The shop doesn't close 'til 5.30pm but I am rotared to finish at 5pm, which suits me fine. Five o'clock is beer o'clock I reckon so I go just around the corner to The Queens Hotel. This is a good real ale pub and I get a pint of Thwaites Wainwright golden beer. It's fairly busy in this lounge bar but I'm lucky to get a seat right by the window onto the busy street, where I can watch the hordes go by. I put my pint on an interesting-shaped beer mat advertising the beer that I'm drinking: Wainwright – 'A breath of fresh ale'. It takes its name from the old guidebook writer AW, who grew up in Blackburn, the home of Thwaites Brewery. The beermat depicts a mountain biker and a quote by AW: *You were made to soar, to crash to earth, then to rise and soar again.* I turn the mat over and on the back there's some wording as follows: *There's nothing quite as exhilarating as facing down and conquering life's mountains. Smashing your best time on the downhill run. Planning your escape from the 'nine-to-five'. Moving to the back of beyond to write your novel. Whatever your personal challenge, why not take a leaf out of Alfred Wainwright's book when facing it? The pioneer of striding confidently off the beaten track and mapping one's own personal path, he was the life-force and inspiration behind this unique golden beer.* Good old AW – yes, he was a pioneer and an inspiration for me. That idea of going away somewhere to write a novel makes me smile. It's something that I've done myself numerous times before, and may do again. And it's a popular romantic idea – the *retreat* from the world to somewhere rural, remote, *wild* to do some creative or recreational challenge, then the triumphant return to society, having achieved something valuable, a 'transformative experience' perhaps that might just enable the person to live more wisely or abundantly.

Checking my watch I see it's now 5.15pm. I'm going to meet someone at 5.30pm to look at a room, so I've got ten minutes to enjoy the rest of this pint and contemplate the world outside this window. The beer is 'lightly hopped, with subtle sweet notes and a delicate citrus aroma', as described on the back of the mat. It's 'the perfectly refreshing reward for those who think they've earned it'. Have I earned it? Yes, I think I have. I drink it down slowly and steadily, get up to return the glass to the bar, then head off up North Road, then up Fair View Road to the house, which is just below the old St. Anne's Church. This would be a great location to live – just up from the Golden Rule, close to the town centre but far enough away from it, a nice quiet corner.

Knocking on the door I am greeted by Phil and Amy, the youngish couple who own the house and who are letting the room. They live here too, but they say they are out for most of the time. They run a café in the village, and also do quite a lot of outside catering. She shows me to the room and it's a poky dimly-lit box that smells of damp. There's a single bed, a wardrobe, a chest of drawers, and not much room for anything else. The first thing I think of is 'Would it make a good room to write?' and the answer is a definite 'No'. There wouldn't be enough room to put all my stuff, never mind set up a writing desk. 'Would there be any storage space anywhere?' I ask. She shows me a cupboard under the stairs that is already full of stuff and says she could move some out to make a bit of room. The kitchen is large and I would be sharing with just the two of them, but they sometimes use it to make large batches of things for the catering business. The shared bathroom is okay. The rent they are asking - £400 per calendar month all-inclusive is too much, although they might well point out that it's the going rate for such a room in Ambleside. I say I'll think about it.

Back at camp I light a fire, but it takes a while to get going because the logs are damp. At least it's stopped raining now. I put the radio on and put a pan of rice and water on to boil. I'm feeling physically tired now from yesterday's big run and I'm happy just to sit in the armchair, drink some beer and listen to the Craig Charles show whilst I wait for the rice to cook. And I think about that room in Ambleside. I wasn't impressed at all. It would be just somewhere to sleep and get a shower and cook a meal, but I wouldn't be able to relax there or feel 'at home' there. I can't afford it anyway because I'd need to find £400 in rent plus a £400 deposit. I'm not even working full-time at the shop and I don't want to be there at all anymore. So the room is a non-starter and I'll hand in a week's notice at the shop tomorrow, even though I've no other job lined up.

The rice is on a slow simmer and the water is nearly all absorbed now, so I open a can of veggie chilli and put that on to heat on the other stove. It feels sad to be eating chilli out of a can, but it's convenient and I can't be bothered cooking tonight. I do enjoy cooking and one of the down sides of this camping life is not having a proper kitchen, which would make cooking proper meals a whole lot easier, but hey ho, this is how it has to be for the time being – the lone wolf in the wood with his tin of beans and his tins of beer, and with a fire and radio for company. I could've got married and had kids and settled down in a proper house with a proper job, but I guess it wasn't meant to be. I should be grateful for what I have and accept who I am. I'll get washed up and then go to bed early, and be thankful that here in the wood I can relax and feel 'at home'. And I don't even have to pay any rent.

Red in Tooth and Claw

A few days later it's a calm sunny morning and I'm sitting in the armchair under the tarp, enjoying doing nothing. A little green caterpillar crawls along the arm of my chair. The spiky feet at the front of its body scuttle along the polyester fabric, then it drags the rear of its body along, arching its back in the middle as it does so. There are lots of these caterpillars at the moment. They seem attracted to the chair and to me. I've just brushed one off my fleece as it was arching its way towards my face.

There are so many 'creepy-crawlies' in this wood – insects of all kinds flying and crawling about. Green flies crawl over my trouser leg and over the white page of my notebook. A fly buzzes around my head, then lands on my hand. A bee gathers pollen or nectar from a nearby blue flower (not a bluebell but something else, I know not what). And down beside my chair, in my washing up bowl of pots and pans, two green spiders have fallen into my stainless steel pan and are trying to make their way out up the smooth curved metal surface, but are unable to get a purchase. One of them seems to have given up now and is still, resting.

But the other one keeps going round or across the bottom of the pan, trying different places to climb the steel wall, but all to no avail. I feel for this spider because I feel I can't get a foothold anywhere in the Lakes anymore, though I keep trying – trying different jobs and trying to find an affordable place to live, but it seems increasingly impossible. I'm priced out of the market for accommodation and I've done just about every job that is possible here and I don't like any of them. Anyway, I'll release the spiders into their natural environment and put the bowl of pans into the car.

Last night I was washing up at the Outgate. I was out the back in the beer garden on my break, having something to eat, and it was busy on the other tables with families. At one of the tables one of the young kids was throwing a tantrum because he couldn't see why they had to sit and eat outside – where there were flies. I didn't think there were that many flies but the poor kid found them really off-putting. He started shouting and crying and threw some of his food on the floor. He was acting like a toddler, though he was a bit older than that. The kids of today seem to take longer to grow up, and some of them never grow up. The father took him away to remonstrate with him, pinning him to the wall by the entrance to the kitchen. I felt sorry for the kid. He might have been pathetic to complain about the flies, but now he was being publicly bullied and humiliated by his father.

Anyway, I wondered how he would get on with all the insects in the wood. It would probably be a nightmare for him. Many kids of today are brought up sealed off from Nature, at home or in school, in some sort of box, a nice clean centrally-heated building with all the windows firmly closed to keep any insects out. Nature might be mediated by a computer or television screen, and there's a show that has celebrities staying in a forest full of creepy-crawlies and the situation is presented as some kind of nightmarish challenge and maybe they even have to eat these insects. Most people aren't keen on insects getting too close to them, but they are an important part of the web of life, the food chain, and as their numbers die off (and I recently read that something like three quarters of all flying insects have died off since 1945), so too do the numbers of birds who feed on them. The world of insects is the same world as the world of birds and the world of humans. Insects may seem 'alien', but they are fellow creatures in our one world.

Anyway, it's nearly time for me to head into town for my last-but-one shift at the shop, followed by another washing up shift at The Outgate. I drink the last of the coffee in my green mug and then get up to brush my teeth, using the last of the water in one of my Nalgene litre water bottles. And as I brush away and then spit into the long grass by the dead beech tree I notice a speck of dirt on my left forearm. I brush it with my right hand but it stays there and almost feels like a little thorn sticking out. I get my specs for a closer look and lo and behold it's a tiny tick. Damn! I've been lucky so far but camping in this wood it's inevitable that I would pick up a tick or two at some point. I spray Smidge repellent onto my lower legs and arms every day and perhaps it's been doing its job well up until now, which is to say I've been tick-free for all these weeks. Oh well, it's not the end of the world, but there is that fear of infection with Lyme disease. I get my special tick tweezers and carefully push the fine curved tines under the body of the tick to gently grasp it as close to my skin as possible, and then pull so that the thing comes out cleanly and drops to the ground. I can't see where it's landed and so I stamp all over the general area in the hope of killing it, so that it doesn't come back for more. And I reflect on the irony of this, having just been talking about the fear of insects. They may be 'fellow creatures' and 'the Lord God made them all', but Nature is also 'red in tooth and claw' and nobody wants a potentially infected parasite biting into you to suck your blood.

Make Time for Poetry

And nobody wants to have their blood sucked out of them by doing a stupid job, but hey ho, it's off to work I go. Jump in the car, drive into Ambleside, earn a few quid. I slide a cassette tape into the slot, and it's New Order and their *Get Ready* album. Bernard Sumner sings of how he doesn't want to be like other people are, doesn't want to own a key, doesn't want to wash his car. He doesn't want to work, like other people do, he wants to be free, he wants to be true.

Managing the shop today is a chap called Martin, who sometimes travels in from Manchester to cover for Sharon's days off (there being currently no supervisor to do that), and he's a nice laid-back guy who's more pleasant to work with than Sharon. There should also be a young lass called Gemma in today, but she's phoned in sick and so it's just myself and Martin. He doesn't understand how I can just jack in my job at the shop and have nothing to go to except for my two evenings a week washing up at the pub. I suppose it does seem reckless, but the truth is I can't stand the shop anymore and I'm just going to trust to luck that I will find something else – trust that 'the wheel of chance will turn my way', as Sumner might say. I'd rather kill myself trying to live than succumb to a living death. Perhaps some other opportunity will present itself, and if not then I could always hang myself from a tree.

Martin states his commonplace worldly philosophy that 'Life is all about earning money to make yourself comfortable.' And of course on one level he is right, and perhaps I am stupid to be asking more of life. Perhaps I should've settled for less. I am, after all, of working-class origin, so why couldn't I have just stuck at a job and earned sufficient money to make myself materially comfortable? Who do I think I am? Perhaps I got ideas above my station. Perhaps I read too many books. Please sir, can I have some more? More of *what* exactly? Well, I guess a more 'spiritual' life, more meaningful work, a real community, making time for contemplation, for creativity, for poetry. Life should not be just about making money to buy things to make yourself comfortable. We are all on some sort of spiritual journey and we all need to make time for some sort of poetry, for life without poetry is no life at all, it's just being a drone, an automaton. Lord give us this day our daily poetry – so that we might be fully human.

By 'poetry' I mean anything that takes us deeper into life, anything that is transfiguring, anything that is spiritual, pretty much anything that is above and beyond the materialistic getting and spending 'to make yourself comfortable' philosophy. Music, dancing, fell-running, meditation, contemplation and recreation in the great outdoors. These can all be 'poetry'. There's a need to make time for these things, and to make time *every day*. I want to live every day, not to put off living just for days off, holidays, retirement or the afterlife. *Now* is the time to live, not tomorrow, for tomorrow may never come.

The day in the shop passes not too unpleasantly. Martin hasn't put the muzak on, which makes for a nicer atmosphere for a start. He's pretty relaxed and he's not bossing me around too much. He's all for taking it easy himself, and I feel like I'm winding down now that I've only got a couple of days left here. We shake hands at the end of the day as I won't see him again. And then I get in the car to drive back to the wood. I'm working at the Outgate again tonight, but I'll walk there over the fields rather than take the car.

The Stuff of True Survival

Walking over the fields from Loanthwaite Lane is very pleasant in the early evening sun. The lambs are playing – running about and jumping up and down, full of energy and the joy of life. One of then runs up to me out of curiosity but its mother calls it back with a low-pitched 'baa'. And then I go through the gate and round the back of the pub into the beer garden, where I've got five minutes to sit and do nothing before I dive into the sink. It would be nice to just relax in the beer garden with a couple of pints and listen to the birdsong, but there'll be a sink full of dirty pots and pans waiting for me and I'll be stuck in that hot kitchen for at least three and a half hours and I can't say I'm looking forward to it.

Tonight young Billy is standing in for Raz as second chef, which is to say he's helping Kat, who is in charge of the kitchen. He asks me about my living in the wood and says 'Are you like Bear Grylls then?' I say I don't know because I only saw him on television once, but no, I think not. From what I've seen and heard Bear Grylls takes a very militaristic approach to survival in the 'wilderness', pitting himself *against* Nature in that whole egotistical, chest-beating, mountain 'conquering' and immature approach to being in the wild, before inevitably going home to his nice comfortable middle-class house somewhere in south-east England. Also, whilst filming for his show 'Man vs. Wild' many of the scenes were staged and he stayed in hotels some nights whilst pretending to be surviving in the wild, on one show when he was supposed to be stranded on a deserted island. He's playing at it in other words, even faking it sometimes, performing for a camera and, of course, for money. So no, I am not like Bear Grylls. I am living in the woods because I don't have much choice, because I am essentially homeless, and although it is challenging I do enjoy the deep connection with Nature that it gives and don't just see it as an arena for showing off my survival skills. I'm not playing at it because this is my only 'home'. I tell Billy as much and I'm surprised when he seems to take personal offence at my criticism of the TV celebrity, who he seems to think is some kind of hero (because of course that's what he's been told to think). 'Oh but you should watch it,' he says. But of course I won't be watching it because I don't have a television, and even if I did I wouldn't be interested anyway. People who enjoy some television programme or film always think that you should watch it and enjoy it too. People who watch a lot of TV and movies relate everything in the real world to what they've seen on a screen. So many times I've heard people, when describing a landscape, say 'It's like something out of *Lord of the Rings*.' When you tell them that you've never seen the film they can hardly believe it and insist that you really *should* see it. But I have no interest in movies, especially not fantasies.

A film crew has been in the area recently, filming for a movie about Beatrix Potter's Peter Rabbit. They actually closed the Wray road at times for a few days whilst they were filming. I was cycling home from Ambleside and was stopped by a man in a high-viz jacket and a walkie-talkie. He said I had to stop and wait for the filming to finish. I did as he said, but I wish I'd told him where to go and cycled through. The film company may have paid for a temporary road closure, but they can't really stop people going about their business, travelling to and from home. They can *ask* people to stop and wait, that's all. There is this presumption that people will comply with the road closures because most people respect the world of big movies and big money – but I don't.

After half an hour or so I've cleared the backlog in the sink and go for my food break – a piece of quiche with a big salad and chips, which I eat sitting on a stool at the back door since the beer garden has now filled up with customers having drinks and looking at menus. The meal orders are starting to come in thick and fast, so I'd better not take too long over my break. It's a nice meal and I'm grateful for Kat's generosity, but it's a pity I can't really relax with it. Back in the kitchen there are now a lot of checks on the tab-grabber and Kat and Billy have got a lot to do. I've done pub-cheffing myself many years ago and it's quite a stressful, demanding job and I wouldn't want to do it again. I have no interest in meat cookery anyway, so it would be purely an exercise in co-ordination and presentation of stuff that mostly means nothing to me. Kat and Billy banter continually, and sometimes it develops into an argument, though it's usually good-natured. Greasy frying pans come my way and as they put them in the sink they warn 'Hot going in!' The swing door opens and Zoe brings in a pile of dirty plates and cutlery, but she's no time to scrape the leftover food into the bin because there's more food under the hot lamps, ready to go out.

And so it goes – a busy evening of relentless washing up. I find myself getting tired and fed up of it all. I feel like jacking in this job too, but I need to keep going with it because I need some money coming in. Never mind Bear Grylls, *this* is the stuff of true 'survival'. Finally, at 9.45pm I take out the bins and sweep and mop the floor. And then I note my time on the time sheet and then have a quick pint at the bar. I've been looking forward to a beer all evening and it goes down well, although there's no-one to chat to because all the staff and customers have gone now at 10pm and Kat is busy doing her food orders.

After my pint I walk across the fields and it feels surprisingly cold after the hot kitchen. I don't know if it's just the contrast or if the temperature has really dropped, but it's amazing how up and down the weather is in the Lakes. One day wet, the next dry, one day warm, the next cold. Last week it was something like 15° in the night and I had to sleep with just a sheet over me, but last night it felt more like about 5°. As I walk up the lane I see my shadow in front of me, cast by the light of just a quarter crescent moon. When I get back to camp I read some of Thoreau's *Walden* by the light of my head torch, sitting under the tarp with a can of beer. But I feel cold and tired and it's getting late, so after only about twenty minutes I decide to call it a day and go to bed, putting on my thermal top and bottoms before getting under the duvet.

Feel Trapped Here Now

Sitting under the tarp, it's raining. A quad bike growls around the fields. Wood-pigeon coo-coos. It was a wet night, but I slept well. Awoke to the sound of a bellowing cow at 7.15am and lay in bed for a while listening to the patter of rain on the tent and the constant running water in the beck. And then – a whoosh of wind coming through the trees lasting several seconds, getting unnervingly louder, until it passed over. I got up and walked down the muddy path to the beck, where I stood on the 'beach' and washed my face. Back to camp: kettle on, breakfast box out of the storage tent and notebook and pen out of the rucksack. And as I sit quietly in my armchair, feeling despondent about the weather and waiting for the kettle to boil for my coffee – a crack from above, something falling through the trees and THUMP! as a dead branch hits the ground just twelve feet away. I get up to investigate. It's just a small branch, little more than a stick, covered in damp moss and also a crust of light-green lichen, half-dead I guess, a superfluous part shed, or rather removed by the wind and the soaking rain. This rain makes all the branches sag so that I have to stoop, and I often bump my head on the low beech branches outside the tent. I don't know where the fallen branch has come from. There are no leaves on it so I can't identify it but I think it's probably from the big oak tree, the trunk of which is some distance away, but whose branches reach out a long way and interweave with those of the beech, ash and hazel.

As I sit in the chair and drink my coffee and write my journal I reflect that falling branches are a hazard of camping in a wood. The rain has stopped and sunshine breaks through the clouds for a few moments. It would be nice to have a settled spell of dry sunny weather, but the pattern for the time being seems to be one of alternating days of sunshine and rain. Oh well, this is the Lake District in August, so it's only to be expected.

It's been a few weeks since I left the job at the shop and I've been enjoying spending more time during the day in the wood, although the weather has been mostly not good. I'm still washing up at the Outgate and have started doing more shifts there, including some daytime food prep, which makes a change from washing up all the time. I've applied for a couple of jobs – one a live-in general assistant position in a hotel and the other working in a warehouse in Kendal. Neither of them appeal very much, but I have to do *some*thing. The hotel job would provide me with a caravan, which would be better than camping in the autumn and winter, but I don't know if I could hack the work. The warehouse job I've done before and it would only be temporary 'til Christmas and tolerable as a temporary measure, but I don't know where I could live in Kendal.

Anyway, I want to enjoy living here in the wood for as long as I can – to make the most of it over what's left of the summer. Sitting in the wood on my own is peaceful. It's a good place to think. I feel at one with the world here. But every time I set off into town I feel irritated by people – by the visitors. It's all couples and families driving round in expensive cars, consuming things. I feel no sense of connection with them. There doesn't seem to be many solitary travellers to the Lake District these days, and few young people 'of limited means', unless they are part of some big organised group. It's all monied people, mostly middle-class. It never used to be like this, but the Lakes has become this place that is all about money and consuming stuff: food, drink, outdoor clothing, visitor attractions and events of one sort or another. To live here with little or no money is to feel an outsider.

I'll go into Ambleside in a bit – to the launderette to tumble dry my damp duvet and pillow, and also to the library to check my email, check the weather forecast, look for jobs and also to write up an account of my Freeman Round for *The Fellrunner* magazine. And then I'm at The Outgate this evening for a washing up shift. But first I need to sort out the contents of my car – whilst the rain has stopped.

Having a car is a bit of a luxury I suppose. Some people manage to wild camp long-term and live just out of a rucksack. That may be the way I end up going, but whilst I've got this car I am grateful for all the space it gives me to store my gear, as well as enabling me to get out and about. I do also have some stuff (my writing desk and chair, some books and files) stored in the barn adjoining the house down the track, but my clothes, my walking, running and cycling gear are all in the back of the car. It's hard keeping it neat and well-organised, but I have to try and keep on top of it so that I can find things. With the back seats folded down there's quite a lot of space, and it's all taken up with plastic crates and dry-bags and bin liners full of clothes for all weathers, plus some books, notebooks, letters, documents, food, sleeping bag etcetera. I sometimes think I should travel more lightly, but all of this stuff is useful and if I didn't have a car to put it in life would be a lot tougher. I spend about half an hour re-arranging stuff and generally putting things in order, taking boxes and bags out of the car and putting them on the roof and bonnet to give me some space so that I can reassemble the jigsaw. But then the rain comes on heavy and I have to get everything in its place quickly. I get into the car and sit in the passenger seat, watching the rain stream down the windscreen. I heave a heavy sigh and wish it didn't rain as much as it does.

In Ambleside library I sit at a computer and do my usual checking of email, Facebook and weather forecasts. The forecast isn't looking good, with lots of rain to come over the next few days and for the foreseeable future. It usually rains a lot in August in the Lakes, but this year seems to be wetter than usual. It makes camping challenging and makes me think about the need to find a room. I search the spare room website but there's very little locally and it's all expensive or for students only. And then I look for jobs and they are nearly all in the 'hospitality' sector. I wonder if I should try for a new life outside of the Lakes and go and live on a community somewhere, so I browse the Diggers and Dreamers website to see what I can find. I could be a volunteer on a community in Dorset or Scotland for a while, but it could only be temporary and inevitably I'd have to return to the Lakes, which is what you might call my 'spiritual home', even though I hate it sometimes. Although I have no actual home here – no house, no physical roots to fix me in a particular place, I do have mental roots, historical roots, spiritual roots that go deep into the landscape, the towns and villages and people of the Lake District. Going away to a different part of the country could be refreshing and give a new perspective, but a return to the Lakes is as inevitable as a migrating bird that comes back home to roost in the familiar place. The Lakeland landscape is in my soul and there is no other that can compare – although having said that, I could do with an adventure elsewhere.

I look out the window and it's pissing down with rain. The thought of going back to camp in the wood is depressing. I type up my account of the Freeman Round and email it to the editor of *The Fellrunner* magazine. And then I log into Facebook and scroll through all the postings – photos of people having a good time on some foreign holiday, pictures of mountains and glasses of beer and plates of food, videos of animals and people doing daft things, some political stuff and online petitions by Greenpeace or whoever, and some music that a friend wants to share with us (although there is no audio facility on this library computer). And what's this here – my old friend Rob Kneebone in Cornwall has shared a posting about the anniversary of the death in August 2010 of one Hope Bourne, an artist and writer who lived simply and almost self-sufficiently in a caravan on Exmoor, growing her own veg, fishing and hunting rabbits with her gun, helping her farmer friends, walking, painting, writing and championing wild places over modern, urban, industrialised and tamed living. She said: *I can't stand towns. I see all the little houses like boxes and everything planned out, laid out, safe and ordered – well there's no adventure in it, no excitement, no anything.* And: *For money you sell the hours and the days of your life, which are the only true wealth you have. You sell the sunshine, the dawn and the dusk, the moon and the stars, the wind and the rain, the green fields and the flowers, the rivers and the sweet fresh air. You sell health and joy and freedom.*

She sounds like a kindred spirit, and I order one of her books, *Wild Harvest*, from Chris at the counter, then go back to the launderette to get my bedding from the tumble drier. The rain is still pouring down and I don't feel like going back to the wood so I set off in the car towards Windermere and Kendal. I want to go to Kendal just to get away from the crowds of the Lakes for a while, and I'm grateful that I have this car. But the traffic is very busy and slow-moving on the A591. There are some massive puddles on the road and the traffic is just crawling along. After fifteen minutes I've only travelled two miles and I decide to turn back to Ambleside. I feel trapped here now. I get a sandwich from the Picnic Box and sit in the car to eat it. The streets are crowded, the cafés are crowded, the shops are crowded. It's high season, the school holidays, the 'silly season'. I could do with a pint so I go up to the Rule but it's absolutely jam-packed with people – walkers in dripping waterproofs, lots of noisy conversation and nowhere to sit, so I give up on that idea and walk back to the car and set off back on the A593 Coniston road. As I approach the turn off for Hawkshead at Brathay I decide to carry on towards Coniston. I'm not sure where I'm going but I'm looking for a quiet pub where I can just sit on my own and read for a while with a couple of good pints of real ale.

In Coniston I look in at The Black Bull and The Crown, but they are both really busy so I carry on down the road to the south end of the village, where I park up at the Ship Inn. It's a Robinson's house, so I get a pint of XB at the bar and sit in the lounge area, which is full of a group of walkers who all know each other and are chatting away noisily and looking at menus. It's only 4.30pm but they are looking to get a meal. I feel out of place, on my own, the loner nursing his pint, unable to relax, no connection with these people. It's a public house but I feel like I'm gate-crashing a private party. This is no place to sit and read. I feel like I'm some kind of outsider or weirdo just for being on my own. Everyone is expected to be in a couple, a family or a group these days in the Lakes. I drink up and go.

It's still pissing down with rain, and I wonder what to do, where to go next – right now, and in my life in general. Despite what I said about the Lakes being my spiritual home, I feel the need to get away for an adventure elsewhere. I'm stuck in that tired old Lakeland loop again, unhappy with everything. I feel trapped. And the thought of going back to my sodden camp depresses me. I drive over Hawkshead Hill and then up Loanthwaite Lane, but carry on past the track to the wood and then take the Wray road to the National Trust campsite. I drive up to one of the toilet blocks because I'm going to have a shower. The campsite is full, mainly with families, and the toilets and showers are busy. I go for a pee in a urinal and the guy at the adjacent one fiddles with his smartphone with one hand, whilst holding himself with the other. Then another guy comes in with his dog and he goes into a cubicle, taking his dog with him. People can't be separated from their mobiles or their dogs, even whilst going to the toilet.

I get a shower and set off in the car again for Ambleside. As I drive through the campsite I note all the expensive cars here – flash BMWs and Audis and Range Rovers, some with personalised number plates, and it's clear that the average camper here nowadays belongs to the affluent classes. Most tents are big expensive things too, and with everything but the kitchen sink. I would hate to camp somewhere like this. It's so busy and noisy with dogs barking and kids running around. Maybe I'm just a grumpy old man, but now I'm looking forward to getting back to my solitary damp camp in the wood, despite the rain. But first I'll go into Ambleside, to the chippy.

At The Walnut I sit and eat my fish and chips inside. It's very busy, but I manage to find a table in the corner. The staff are friendly and they are getting to know my face now that I'm something of a regular here. I never used to eat chips so much before I started this camping life, but it seems like the best thing on a wet evening like this, when trying to cook up some sort of hot meal on a camping stove would be very challenging and depressing. Here it is warm and dry and I've got a good plateful of hot, highly calorific food.

Driving back to camp with a full belly I'm feeling a bit better about life. Simple things can make a big difference. But when I get back to the wood my heart sinks as I see the ground is waterlogged and there are some big puddles. The beck is a torrent, the water running over the top of my stepping stones, but not so deep that I can't still step on the stones to get across. I'm wearing my old Goretex boots, but one of them seems to have sprung a leak in the forefoot. I can't afford a new pair of boots for the time being so I'll just have to live with it. My camp is well situated, being on a patch of high ground above the beck, and although the ground is sodden, it's not going to flood here. The tarp is sagging with a big pool of water in the middle so I lift it up for the water to run off the back. The cardboard flooring is completely sodden, and as I walk over it my feet sink through the disintegrating material into a sloppy brown mud.

The soaked beech branches are all sagging low so that I have to stoop as I make my way to the sleeping tent, where I see a branch lying right beside it. One end has a sharp edge, and I notice that there's a small cut in the flysheet fabric near the bottom. My first thoughts are that I suspect foul play from Dorothy's helper Harry, who I know doesn't like me, and doesn't like me being here in the wood. He thinks he rules the roost at the house now, and no doubt he resents the fact that I'm living here rent-free and not doing any jobs at the house, even though I don't use it anymore. But then I realise that the branch probably fell from a nearby tree. There are two other branches, about three to four feet long, lying over the guy line and the shoulder of fabric at the low end of the tent, and it was probably one big branch that broke into three when it hit the ground. It's lucky that it wasn't a bigger branch, and that I wasn't in the tent at the time. Anyway, the branch coming down reminds me of this hazard of camping in the wood, and it gets me thinking that maybe it's a sign that my time is coming to leave this place.

Inside the tent the groundsheet feels damp and I could do with drying it out when we get a dry weather day. The woollen blanket also feels damp and the whole tent smells of damp – damp fabrics, damp earth, and also the acrid smell of mulched grass and leaf mould beneath the groundsheet. The groundsheet lies on top of a plastic tarp, which should be impermeable to water, but water has obviously found its way in between the layers. Anyway, I reinstate my bed with the tumble-dried duvet and pillow, which

I've brought from the car inside a black bin liner. And once I'm under the duvet I feel cosy and warm and dry, despite the ambient dampness. I put in my ear plugs and soon fall asleep.

Despondent and Sluggish

This morning I awoke to rain hammering on the flysheet and the sound of the beck in spate. It must've been a very wet night. I got up very early to go for a pee and saw a big fat slug on the inside of the tent door, by the zip. I slid it into the plastic container I use for this purpose and threw it into the sodden undergrowth. And then I put my bare feet into my damp boots, which I keep in the porch area in a boot bag. I started keeping them in a bag to stop slugs crawling into them. One day I discovered that I'd been walking round in my boots with a squashed slug under my heel. I only found out when I took the boots off in the afternoon and saw a big mess of slime on the insole and the heel of my sock. I wondered what it was at first, then realised it was a flattened slug, no skeleton obviously, or even any recognisable shape, just a very sticky mess. I still check my boots for slugs when I take them out the bag, and there were none this morning. But as I stood by the fireplace, pissing into the long grass in the half-light and the pissing rain, I felt something crawling over my foot inside my right boot. I quickly took the boot off and shook out a beetle, hopping on my other foot, cursing and losing my balance so that my bare foot came down into the mud to stop myself from falling over.

Now as I write, sitting under the tarp, my plastic mug of steaming coffee on the table, the rain is easing off a bit, although probably only temporarily. The air is still and there are quite a few midges about. I get the Smidge repellent and spray some on my forearms and ankles, and also smear some around my neck. I'm depressed with this camping life, but what is the alternative right now? There's a puddle of rainwater on the cardboard at my feet and this cardboard is pretty useless in the rain. The carpet was better, but I got rid of that after it got sodden and muddy after several weeks' use. Nothing is going to be effective against this rain and mud, except perhaps for some wooden decking, but this is not suburbia, this is a transient camp, even if it is dragging on a bit. When I leave this place I should leave no trace that I was here – except for the fireplace ring of stones. I walk, bent over beneath the sodden sagging branches, and I feel cowed by the weather, reduced to a stoop, grovelling about in the rain and mud and not enjoying being here at all – just surviving and hoping for better days to come, although the forecast is bad for another whole day and evening. The drying out of the tent will have to wait. The cardboard disintegrates beneath my feet as I walk and slide down the steep path down the bank to the beck. I've roughly bedded in a few flat rocks as steps here, but two of them slide away under my feet in the mud. At the beck the beach is submerged as well as the stepping stones. I splash some cold water on my face for a wash, then struggle back up the muddy bank to get back under the shelter of the sagging tarp.

What shall I do with myself today? Take sanctuary in the public library probably. There's another guy who's wild camping who goes in there most days and he likes to talk and complain about his lot. Apparently his wife kicked him out of his house and now he camps on Loughrigg with his dog. He's trying to get a job and a room but that's going to be difficult with him having a dog. I'll chat to Chris, the librarian, get a coffee, go on the internet, read a bit. I'll get a sandwich from the Picnic Box, then later this afternoon I've got a shift at The Outgate. But before I leave Ambleside I must remember to get some fresh cardboard from the recycling bin.

The rain eases off a bit and I decide to walk down the track to get a bigger view. I have to cross the stream at another point, where it's narrower. The ground is puddled and very muddy, but I manage to find a route on relatively firm ground. Walking down the track I notice that the water-filled potholes have got deeper and need repairing again. I emerge from the trees for the bigger picture but all I can see is a grey blanket of cloud right down to valley level, with even the tops of the trees obscured. I feel despondent and sluggish – not that I want to liken myself to slugs. There are lots of them about this morning on the track, as they like these damp conditions. Sometimes there are loads of them on the tent, as if they are attracted to the texture of the polyester. They also seem to like to place themselves right by the zip of the door so that I have to be careful when I'm in and out not to brush them off onto me. It has happened once or twice and there's something horrible, something disgusting about the cold slimy things on your skin. You brush them off and they leave a little slimy patch behind. There are often slimy trails all over the flysheet, pearlescent and pretty in a certain light, if you don't see the ugly creatures that have made them. Some slugs are shiny liquorice-black, some are a sickly-looking orange colour, and some are tiny baby slugs that aren't easy to spot sometimes. I'm very careful not to keep the door of the tent open for long as the last thing I want is to share my bed with slugs.

I walk back up the track to the camp and sit under the tarp. It feels quite cold, and although it's only mid-August it feels like the beginning of autumn. Over in the field sheep have started bleating pitifully, and then I hear the quad bike growling round. Sometimes sheep escape from the field and come down the track to the house, where they find all sorts of treats in the garden – which of course Dorothy isn't happy about, but you can't blame the sheep and you've got to admire their adventurous spirit. They are always finding ways of escape from their fenced-in field. Domesticated 'livestock' they may be, but they are also wilful and wily creatures who enjoy a bit of adventure, and the grass is generally greener on the other side of the fence, but they always return to their heaf or home field – back to the familiarity of flock and fold.

No Shepherd, No Priest, No Masters

Sun-dappled oak trunk, the cooing of wood pigeons. What am I to do with my life in the world of jobs? If I can keep writing, keep my inner poet alive and keep being enchanted by Nature then perhaps I can find a way to survive. It's a cool dry morning, gentle breeze and sunlight coming through the trees. My morning coffee sits in a green plastic mug on the small wooden table whilst I sit in my chair beneath the tarp with my notebook and pen.

It's a cold autumnal morning, sunlight coming through the trees, the sound of a big waggon on the Hawkshead road half a mile away. It's September and it's surprising how quickly the days are shortening. It's going darker earlier in the evenings and at 6am this morning it was only just beginning to get light in the wood. Now at 7am it's still not fully light, and only just light enough to write these words without the aid of a lamp. I'll take a walk down the track to the house to get a view of the sky and the fells.

August was a wet month, but it's been a few weeks since that very wet spell when I thought I'd have to leave the wood, not that I had anywhere to go. I finally managed to get the tent groundsheet dried out by hanging it on a line down at the house on a dry sunny day. That tear in the flysheet didn't get any worse and I repaired it with duct tape. The last week or so has been quite dry and sunny – almost what you might call an Indian summer. But autumn is definitely on the way and more and more leaves on the trees are turning yellow and brown.

As I walk down the track a slight breeze causes some yellow birch leaves to fall slowly to the ground like confetti. Then as I emerge into the open I get the big view: Light-grey cloud, slow-moving, just clipping the top of Coniston Old Man but down over Fairfield. There are also some patches of blue, and the weather forecast is for it to be dry and sunny, once this cloud lifts. I'm planning for a day out in North Lakes, where I'm going to do the Dale Head fell race this afternoon. I've been doing quite a lot of running lately, with not working at the shop, and it will be good to push myself with a race, and also have a bit of social. I've got to make the most of what time I've got left, and enjoy the good weather whilst I can. I walk back up the track, into the wood and put the kettle on.

I've also got a job interview for a position of general assistant at a hotel in Braithwaite later this morning. My money is fast running out and I need to get a full-time job soon. I'm still working at the Outgate a couple of evenings a week, but that's barely enough to keep me in food, beer and petrol, and I have some car expenses coming up and some small debts to pay off. I look at my watch: 7.20am. And I watch the kettle coming up to boil – steaming, and starting to whistle. I've got a couple of hours to kill, or rather to spend as best I can.

At 7.30am the sound of a mechanical digger in the distance, its big metal digging bucket rattling noisily. My heart sinks. It must be at least half a mile away, but the noise really carries and I don't want to hear industrial sounds in my woodland idyll. It's probably doing groundworks for further development of holiday lodges on the edge of Hawkshead village. There's always someone in a mechanical digger around Hawkshead. The noise started at 7.30am yesterday too, and went on until 7.30 in the evening. Someone working long hours in the service of some money-making venture. Cumbrians are grafters, being hard-working for the sake of being hard-working – keeping busy as if busyness is somehow next to godliness. People are so eager to turn themselves into robots, especially for the god of money.

Yeah, sure we all need money, we've all got to eat, got bills to pay etc., but if every day consists merely of long hours of toil, re-fuelling and resting, then we are not really living. Living for a holiday or retirement or an afterlife is not really living at all. A life fully lived is a life lived every day, and every day should include some recreation, some reflection, some creativity, some play. All work and no play makes Jack a dull boy, and this world is full of hard-working dull Jacks and Jills.

But this morning the digger sound only lasts a few minutes. Perhaps the operator drove off to do some digging elsewhere. And I can relax in the wood, listening to the peaceful sound of a wood pigeon coo-cooing – not one, but two coo-cooing to each other. I sit and stare into the trees for a while, doing nothing but listening and watching. A squirrel scampers along the ground then up a hazel tree – perhaps to get some nuts. A wasp buzzes around and is attracted to my plastic bag bin, which hangs from a stake at the edge of the tarp. It can probably smell the banana skin in there. On the ground there aren't quite so many slugs as there were, but some little snails have arrived. Unto every thing a season. I drink some coffee, then set off through the trees to go for a shit and to get some firewood. As I make my way to the toilet area I brush through tendrils like tangled hair dangling from the branches, but the smell of honeysuckle is long gone.

After emptying my bowel into yet another little grave marked by a cross of twigs I drag a dead beech branch back to camp. I saw it up into small logs, which I place side by side on a slate plinth by the fireplace. I arrange them so that they overhang the slate to rest on a log beside it, so that there's some space underneath. And now I've got myself a xylophone. I strike the log-keys with another small log and they make a pleasing noise, each with its own pitch.

I've got plenty of logs for a fire tonight, but I could do with some kindling so I set off to do some foraging, and I don't have to go far. Over by the beck I gently shake a bendy young living hazel and a load of yellow leaves fall into the running water. Beside it there's a dead pole, about twelve feet tall and bereft of living shoots or leaves. I snap it easily at its moss-covered base and carry it back to camp, where I snap it into good firewood lengths. The wood snaps with a loud healthy crack – not rotten and not too green but just about right. I just have to use the bow saw at the thicker end. And then I pick up all my pale kindling sticks and stow them neatly under the table under the tarp, where they look like a bunch of giant breadsticks.

It's now 10am and bells ring out from the church in Hawkshead, summoning the flock to morning service. A quad bike growls haltingly round the fields, the farmer checking on his own flock. I am not one of either church flock or field flock. I am the lone fox in the woods, with no shepherd, no priest, no masters. I am outside the gate, beyond the intake wall. Nature is my church, whether it be woods or fells. The sun is shining through the trees, the wood is warming up and it's shaping up to be a beautiful day. It's time I got in the car and headed up to Braithwaite for my job interview and then the fell race later. And I look forward to getting up onto the fell to re-create, to re-wild and to re-find the deep spiritual connection that sustains me.

But can that really sustain me? It may be food for the soul, but I also need real food to eat, and also shelter and social life. I need a job of some sort if I am to survive, but if that job requires me to turn myself into a robot or to work for some corporate money-making machine whose values mean nothing to me then I have to ask myself: Is survival really worth it?

A Place of Pagan Worship

At the hotel I am greeted by the owner, a burly chap in his sixties, with a limp and with a grizzled and fierce look about him. He bids me sit down in the lounge area and he goes off to get me a coffee, and then comes back with his wife to interview me. And so the interview begins, quite formal, and I feel pretty uncomfortable. The guy doesn't exactly put me at ease. And I have to talk about my previous work experience and how it would relate to the job of general assistant here. I'd be doing a mixture of waiting tables in the restaurant, pulling pints behind the bar and helping in the kitchen. I'm not sure I'll be up to it, but I'll have to give it a go. It's many years since I worked as a waiter, and I don't relish the prospect of all that running round at everyone's beck and call, asking them if they're enjoying their meals, then clearing their plates and asking them if they want to see the dessert menu. It's all a sort of formalised game that's not really my thing. I think I'd rather be behind the bar or washing up, but I've got to be flexible. The old guy emphasises that he doesn't want me to see the position as a 'launch pad' for something else in the area – he wants someone who's going to stick at the job long-term. He gives me a piercing look, as if to ascertain whether I'm a restless wanderer, or if I'd be a loyal and committed servant. I say I'd have to see how it goes, but that I have no plans to do anything else, which is not untrue. His wife then shows me to the caravan, which would be my accommodation. It's a decent size, with its own little kitchen and shower and second bedroom, which I wonder if I could use as a writing room once all the junk in there has been moved out. They wouldn't want much rent for the caravan either – just £30 a week. But one potential problem I can foresee is the two collie dogs running around in the compound which is immediately adjacent. They are friendly enough but I am told they are 'guard dogs', and whilst we look around the caravan they have a session of loud barking as some people walk along the nearby footpath to the hotel. We go back into the hotel where I have another brief chat with the old guy and then we say we'll both think about it and then get back to each other.

I've got some time to kill, so I go for a little walk through the village and then take the path towards Newlands that skirts the edge of the open fell. It's quite a pleasant walk, although the bracken is thick and high on both sides of the path. On my right is the steep slope of Barrow, and on my left is an interesting-looking wood that rises up to a small rounded hill or 'how'. I decide to climb over the barbed wire fence to go and explore what could be a good area for a wild camp. There are a few pheasants strutting about and I get the impression that this is one of those woods that's used simply for rearing and shooting them. I climb up a steep slope through pine trees and reach the top of the hill, where there's a cluster of yews. On the ground, half buried, there's an old shotgun cartridge, the metal end gone rusty. I keep walking to the highest point, where there's a nice little clearing beneath some yews – a perfect-looking camping spot. And how is it that a stand of yews grows here? Is it a fragment of the ancient wildwood? It seems a strange place to plant yew trees, unless they were planted here to mark some ancient site of pagan worship – which is what yews are often associated with. Christian churches were often built on the same sites, superimposing them and absorbing paganism into Christianity. But this hill would not be a practical place to build a church. Anyway, whether or not it was once a place of pagan worship, it could be anyone's 'church' of nature-worship. Perhaps some places are more sacred than others, but anywhere in Nature is sacred – especially the wild places.

Walking a little further, I'm out of the yews and into an open area of bracken and gorse and with some scattered small birch, and other deciduous trees. The ground slopes down to a farm called Braithwaite Lodge and there's a big view northwards to Skiddaw, and the A66. The road must be about half a mile away but it's still quite noisy, which is a shame. I walk back the way I came, back to the car, and then set off down the road to Borrowdale.

Pushing the Body to its Limit

The Dale Head fell race is usually held in conjunction with the Borrowdale Show or 'Shepherd's Meet', but the show has been cancelled this year because the fields have been waterlogged from the prolonged period of wet weather. But the fell race is still taking place, and it should be pleasantly low-key with there being no show on, and also because it clashes with a popular race elsewhere. I get a parking spot at the designated car park by the Scafell Hotel and then register my entry at the village hall over the road. The entry fee is only three quid and I get my number and pin it to my Ambleside AC vest. There's only one other Ambleside vest here – someone I don't know, but there are a few other people I know from different clubs so there's a bit of chat to be had before we gather on the start line.

And then we're off – the mad charge down the stony track towards the river, then splashing through the water, taking care not to slip on the rounded stones on the riverbed, then alongside the river for a bit, then over a field and up the fell. The start of a short race like this always seems fast and is a shock to the system. But as we head up the steep slope through Rigg Head quarries I can settle into some sort of rhythm. It becomes too steep for running and so everyone is walking now, though still working hard – 'power-walking' I guess you'd call it. In a race that should only take me about an hour there can be no slackening of effort – it's push, push push all the way. But my legs feel strong and I'm moving well, overtaking a few people on this long climb. I feel a core strength that rises to the challenge and I've got the bit between my teeth. The 'sun king' is within me, even though the sun's not shining without any more. At the top of Rigg Head the gradient eases off and we can run again for a few hundred yards – past Dalehead Tarn, and then we start the second big climb up Dale Head. There's very little flat running in this race – just that bit at the start and finish across the valley and beside the river, then this short bit halfway up. At 4.5 miles and 2,215' of climb this is a proper little fell race, a short 'A' category race with more contours to the distance than most fell races.

I'm climbing now alongside Catherine Spurden of Keswick AC. She works at the Longthwaite youth hostel, just down the road – where I used to work about twenty-five years ago. She's a top fell runner and I must be doing well to be keeping up with her, although maybe she's off form at the moment. She keeps making little grunting noises, which sound like grunts of pleasure, as much as from the 'pain' of the exertion. It's not really pain, but it's a pushing of the body to its limit – heart, lungs and legs being pushed as hard as they can go, which is far from comfortable, but is pleasurable in a way. We climb into a thick mist and have to be careful to stay on course as we cut a big corner to the left of the path. And finally we top out over the convex curve and jog together around the trig point, where our race numbers are duly noted and we receive shouts of encouragement – especially Catherine, as she is more well-known than me, plus she's the leading lady in this race.

Back down we go, and we have to take some care to get our line right as we scamper down the bumpy grassy ground, more or less retracing our steps from the climb. This descent has never been easy, no matter how fit I've been, but I do manage to get ahead of Catherine. Down we go, out of the cloud and I can see the way ahead clearly now. It's fast feet down the very steep direct grassy route to the right of the pitched path, then taking care through some rocky stuff and across the flat boggy bit, round a big rock, over the beck, a small climb and then down through the quarries, the clatter of loose slates and trying to remember the quickest route down here. I'm probably taking the 'wrong' path, which is the one I used to take down here on my training runs many years ago, which isn't the quickest, but possibly the most enjoyable way down – on loose slates rather than the hard bedded-down stones of the more direct route. I've got someone chasing me now, a Keswick AC runner, Mike Mallen, who is hot on my heels and who is probably relying on me to lead him down the optimum route, which this isn't.

By the time we hit the grassy path below the quarries a couple of other runners have got ahead of us by taking the quicker route, though Catherine is still behind. And now we can let ourselves go, brakes off and hell for leather for the final mile or so back to the finish. There are a few of us close together now and there can be no let-up in the pace. Push, push all the way, along the river, then splashing through the water again, almost losing my balance at one point, but keeping the forward momentum going – onto the stony track and it's a sprint finish as someone comes past me, but I'm pretty much finished and don't have it in me to chase after him as the red and white tape of the finishing funnel comes into sight and it's cheers and smiles all round.

And what a relief it is to finish – possibly the best bit of the whole thing. A plastic cup of orange juice and some hand-shaking and mutual congratulation, then back to the car to get changed, then to the village hall for a bit of crack and the prize-giving. The winner is young Ted Ferguson and Catherine is the first lady. I placed 13th overall, but only third veteran over 50. I'm glad I came up for the race today – it's been a good day out. Worries about accommodation and jobs have been blasted away and now I feel as calm and peaceful as a buddha. People go their separate ways in their vehicles and I think I'll stop in Ambleside on the way back for some beer and chips.

Landlord John at the Rule insists on buying me a pint, having read my report of the Freeman Round in *The Fellrunner* magazine. I suppose it's a bit of publicity for the pub in that the round starts and finishes there – not that the place needs any more publicity. So I have a convivial couple of pints and then go to the Walnut chippy, where I get a takeaway and sit on the bench in my usual place at the back of the church.

The sun's going down over Loughrigg and it's getting chilly, but I'll get a roaring fire going when I get back to camp. It's the end of summer and change is in the air. I feel that today's fell race was the last one I'll do for a long time, and perhaps I'll never do one again, so I'm glad to end the summer on a good note. My future is uncertain, but today has been a good day and every day counts.

To Be or Not to Be

5.45am. Wood pigeons coo-cooing before it's light. It's dark in fact as I get out of my tent with my head torch on to go for a pee. Perhaps not as dark as it was in the night – perhaps the faintest hint of the sun on its way up. The wood pigeons seem to be calling to each other, three or four of them from different points in the wood. I go back to bed and wait for it to get light, listening to the pigeons. Then I reach for the head torch again and put on my specs to read a bit more of *Walden*, but they instantly steam up, as usual. It's such a humid atmosphere in the tent. It was a warm night – in the teens, I think, and the warmest it's been pretty much all summer, even though it's now autumn. Anyway, reading in the tent is not possible so I just lie here under the damp duvet, waiting for it to get light.

After about three quarters of an hour it's light enough to see what I'm doing without a torch, so I go down to the stream to wash my face and then walk back to dry myself with the towel that hangs on the line, the towel that has taken on the musty smell of damp – a smell I can't get rid of. Another smell in my nostrils this morning is the smell of death, or rather the smell of something dead. At first I thought I was smelling gas and wondered if there was a leak of butane from the stove, but there wasn't, so it must be some dead animal somewhere in the trees, or perhaps in the fields. It smells like dead sheep, but perhaps other dead animals smell similar. On such a still, warm humid morning perhaps the smell of a dead sheep could travel some distance from the fields. It's the time of year for things to be dying off.

Walking down the track I feel a lingering stiffness in my legs from the fell race the day before yesterday. Also a soreness in one of my ankles from an old injury. As you get older it takes longer to recover from the rigours of fell-racing. As I walk some leaves gently fall from the trees. As more and more leaves fall and the branches become bare my camp will become visible from the lane, but I will be gone from here before that happens.

Yesterday morning I was walking across the fields into the village when I came across a crow hanging in a tree from one of its legs, which was caught in some wind-blown plastic netting. It flapped its wings and struggled to break free, but the netting was well wrapped around its leg. I thought about trying to climb the tree to release the bird, but when I looked at the branches I realised it wasn't possible so I had to leave it be, or *not* to be – that was the situation, the inevitability of dying alone, hanging from a tree. It could've been me, and may yet be, hanging from my neck, struggling to break free, despite the act being voluntary. The body would gasp for air and thrash around, struggling for survival, despite my mind having overridden it. Anyway, I took pity on the crow. It had more reason to live than me. Its presence was more justified than mine. No doubt it had a mate, offspring, a community of fellow crows and its natural habitat, whereas I am on my own, without a home. Nothing justifies my presence here anymore, to tell the truth.

I walked on into the village, where I sat outside the Kings Arms and had a solitary pint in the late afternoon sun. I watched the visitors milling around in their fashionable leisure wear and pristine white trainers – overweight people with football tee-shirts and tattoos and dogs of one sort or another. Couples holding hands and looking at menu boards and wondering where to have dinner. One couple were sitting at a table with a bottle of rosé wine in a cooler, their faces looking bored. They had nothing to say to each other and so they stared at and fiddled with their smartphones, scrolling through Facebook or Twitter or whatever. He took a photo of the wine in the cooler to post online, and then there was a series of little electronic noises, presumably as his online friends 'liked' the photo.

Hawkshead is a place where you can eat and drink and look at the quaint buildings. You can buy some fudge and a Barbour jacket and be glad that you've got away for a break from your home town or city. It's another honeypot, another vulgar cash register.

I finished my pint and decided to call at the art gallery across the square, where my old flame Cara works. We had a quick hug and she told me about the paintings she'd sold that day. The artwork in there is not to my taste – mainly tasteless garish colours or photographic-style paintings of landscapes or wildlife. Anyway, I asked her if she'd like to join me for a drink when she finished at 5pm, in ten minutes, but she said she had to rush home and then go to one of her cleaning jobs to make the money she needs to send one of her sons on a school ski-ing holiday. All work and no play makes Cara a dull girl. So I left her to get ready to rush off and went to sit in the churchyard for a bit, to reflect on the love we used to make, for which she's no time anymore. She's so busy trying to make a living there's no time for living itself – for *life*. It's all making money and no making love.

Sitting on the wooden bench with my back to the church I looked at the gravestones in front of me. All these dead people. I wondered how many had led satisfying life-filled lives and how many were slaves to grafting and making money just to survive, or maybe just because they couldn't think of anything better to do with their lives. I remember sitting on that bench with Cara some years ago and we had a long delicious snog, like teenagers. We were in no hurry and just wanted to enjoy each other's' company. Then we set off walking hand in hand over the fields to the bluebell wood, where we made passionate love on the soft grass, under the trees, all of Nature our witness, before continuing our walk to my rented place in High Wray, where we drank some wine and made a nice meal together. That was living. That was feeling alive and enjoying life. Now the pair of us are older, but there's still plenty of living to do, I think – or maybe I'm being over-optimistic.

I walked out of the village to Knipe Fold and on towards Barngates. Now and then a Range Rover or similar vehicle went past, on its way to the Drunken Duck gastro pub perhaps. This is Range Rover territory, an area where people like to drive around in their luxury four-wheel drive vehicles with private number plates and wine and dine, dressed up in their smart casual countrywear. As I neared the Duck I saw an actual duck crossing the road slowly, hesitantly. It looked at me and made little quacking noises, as if appealing for help. One of its wings looked injured and I wondered if it had been hit by one of those 4WD vehicles that was travelling too fast. Anyway I wasn't sure, and there wasn't anything I could do, so I carried on over the crossroads with the intention of finding a path up through the trees onto Black Fell, where I was going to look for a possible wild camping spot. It was an idea I had early on in the season, when I wasn't sure if I was going to be able to stay in the wood for long, and I needed a contingency plan. On the 2½" OS map it looked like a promising area. There was a spring marked near what looked like a flattish area. And beyond that there was a small tarn near a part of the fell called Stephen How. That name appealed to me. If I was to camp up there it would be appropriate. I could re-name it with my own spelling variant of 'Steven How', or maybe 'Steven, Why?' Why? Because I'm desperate. A homeless man seeking some sort of place I can pitch my tent in the fells, somewhere out of the way, outside the gate, away from society. But in bad weather it would be a terrible place to live. At least in the wood I have some degree of shelter from the elements, and also I am hidden from view. The open fell is no place to camp when the weather is bad.

I set off down the Skelwith road towards the track to the fell, but began to realise what a crazy idea it was. It would be a very steep climb up through the trees and I didn't have any energy. In fact I felt weak, lethargic, despondent. I was sick of my homeless life. I turned back to the crossroads and turned left, down the hill to the Outgate Inn, where I called in for a couple of pints in the company of my work colleagues, who weren't too busy at around 4pm, this being the gap period between lunches and dinners. In truth there wasn't much interesting conversation to be had. They were talking about tattoos and betting and the drunken time two of them had at a nightclub in Windermere the previous night. I felt on the outside, but some sort of friendly social interaction was better than none. After two pints of XB I continued my walk over the fields and alongside Blelham Tarn to Low Wray, where I filled my water bottle at the campsite. From there I followed the Wray road for a little way up the hill, then took the path to Tock How, then over the fields, back to the wood.

Today looks like it's going to be another bright and sunny day so I want to go for a walk again somewhere. I'm going to have to get used to walking or cycling everywhere now because the car has broken down. On the way back from Ambleside yesterday morning it ground to a halt just beyond Brathay, just at a bad spot at a bend in the road. I called the breakdown recovery people and when the man finally arrived in his van he told me that the timing belt had gone. So it was pretty much the end of the car, as it would cost way too much to repair. He towed me back to the wood and left it in my usual parking spot under the big old oak tree. I can still use it as a store for my stuff, but it isn't going anywhere anymore, and at some point I'll have to empty it and then get a scrap merchant to tow it away.

Reviving the Fire

Slept soundly last night, despite anxiety over my impending move out of the wood. I decided against the live-in job at the hotel and will instead take up the temporary job at the warehouse in Kendal. An old work colleague and friend has a spare room in his town centre flat, and that's where I'll be moving to. He's coming to collect me in his car in a couple of hours and we'll transfer all my stuff from the dead Peugeot into his vehicle.

Last night I made a good strong fire that stayed in just through the night, and when I got up in the pre-dawn half-light for a pee the remains of the final log were still smouldering red. This was a surprise because it was raining heavily when I went to bed at 10.30pm and must've rained quite a lot in the night. When I got up at 8am the embers had almost died, but I managed to revive the fire with some newspaper, the last of the kindling and some sticks. And for the last hour-and-a-half I've been preoccupied with keeping this little fire going, breaking off for breakfast but then returning to it to re-arrange it and to go into the wood to collect some more sticks, snapping off a few small dead holly branches.

Fire is fascinating and distracting. I remember when I first moved to the Lakes to work at Buttermere Youth Hostel I used to love burning the cardboard boxes in the garden at the back of the hostel. That was in 1987, before the advent of widespread cardboard recycling, and one of the weekly jobs at the hostel was to burn all the empty cardboard boxes we got from food deliveries. I would stand there mesmerised by the flames and the smoke, and also by the great view of the High Stile ridge in the background. There was something about the fire that took me back to the 'primitive' man of my forbears for whom fire was a magical thing that played an important part in survival. It's still a magical thing of course, but something of a novelty for most people, who live on gas and electricity. The warden Tony used to say that there was no need to stand over and watch it for too long – as I was probably needed back in the hostel, but I used to enjoy those moments of just staring at the fire and the mountains, which made a nice distraction from working in the kitchen or cleaning dormitories or whatever other mundane hostel duties I had to do.

This morning the fire is a distraction from all the work I have to do in dismantling the camp and sorting out my stuff in the car to move to Kendal. I've been here in the wood for four-and-a-half months now, and

I'll be sad to leave, even if it has been a bit grim lately with the wet weather – which will only get worse. I have to leave the wood, but I'm not really looking forward to moving to the flat in Kendal as I worry about all the inevitable noise disturbance from living in the centre of the 'auld grey town'.

Perhaps I slept well partly because the fire kept burning overnight and the smell of wood smoke had a relaxing effect. Perhaps just the knowledge that it was burning away into the night, despite the rain, a symbol of life carrying on, against the odds of being doused, still glowing slightly in the morning, a source of light in the dark, heat in the cold – an expression of vitality.

I walk into the trees, carrying a bin bag full of sodden cardboard. The bag is heavy and it's a struggle as I walk away from my usual route, through the thick undergrowth down to a large fallen tree, its root base torn from the ground and exposed in the vertical plane. Below this root base is a hole, where I empty the contents of the bin bag – a mass of wet cardboard, some sheets already half-disintegrated, others still intact and bearing the name of the outdoor shop where I worked. I distribute the cardboard evenly in the hole, then cover it with some small leafy branches, disguising my ugly dump. It will all bio-degrade anyway – it's only wood pulp after all. It originated from a wood, and now it's returning to a wood.

Walking back to camp with the empty bag I now feel the need to empty my bowel, so I get the shovel and head off back into the trees in a different direction – to the usual place. There are many twig crosses on the ground, marking the graves of my deposits, from which I hope the trees and plants will extract some nutritive goodness. I dig a hole, drop my trousers and pants, squat down and excrete another piece of steaming manure, then bury it with the wet earth, finally marking the spot in the usual way, the final grave for my final day here.

As I walk back through the wood I look around at the trees, my neighbours and friends for a season. They have protected me and sustained me, and I am grateful to them. I touch the trunk of the holly and whisper 'thank you', then I do the same with the big oak and the beeches around my camp. And I am once again aware that we are kindred, we are one. I don't really want to leave this wood and live in the middle of town, but I can't stay here any longer. Dorothy wants me out, the weather is driving me out, I'm running out of money and I need full-time paid employment. Alas I must return to civilisation and domestication.

I return to the fire, crouching down by the ring of stones and blowing hard on the wigwam of beech pole sticks and holly kindling. Some of the wood is still quite damp and there's a lot of smoke, which stings my eyes. I reach in to re-arrange the sticks a bit and start blowing again, nursing the red glow and the little flickerings into some vital flames, trying to get this fire to the point where it's got a strong life of its own. It's almost there, I think, as I place a couple of small logs over the sticks and clouds of smoke billow towards me. I stand up, stand back and smile as the flames take hold.

The robin has just come to pay me a visit on my last morning, flitting between the low branches, tweeting and keeping an eye on me. Now I've got to get to work on packing up and leaving this place. Goodbye robin. Thankfully it's not raining now and the sun is starting to break through the grey blanket of cloud.

Lightning Source UK Ltd.
Milton Keynes UK
UKHW012157210922
409216UK00004B/893

9 781527 244412